# THE INTREPID EXPORTER

"The Intrepid Exporter" first published in the U.K. in 2023 by Mike Stokes, Exportential Limited, 13 Beccelm Drive, Crowland, Lincolnshire, PE6 0AG.

E-Mail address : mike.stokes@exportential.co.uk

ISBN  978-1-7393342-1-5

# CONTENTS

# INTRODUCTION

Money isn't everything – usually it isn't even enough. (Anon)

I don't care too much for money. Money can't buy me love. (Lennon & McCartney)

An advertising agency is 85% confusion and 15% commission. (Fred Allen)

Before you start reading this book, you need to understand why I believe I am qualified to teach other people all about exporting. Why exactly should you pay heed to the various pieces of advice given in this book? Without giving you a full autobiography, I'd like to share the journey I have taken in order to build up this wealth of exporting knowledge and experience.

From pre-school days I had always shown a keen interest in geography and maps, encouraged by my father and grandfather. I quickly acquired a sense of where countries were located – relative to the U.K. and to each other. In my teens I passed A levels in Geography and Economic Geography, without realising how handy they would be throughout my working career.

When I left school, I joined the domestic appliance manufacturer, Hotpoint, as a Commercial Apprentice. My four years apprenticeship included block release stints at college as well as hands-on practical experience in the company's various finance and accounting departments – the objective being that I would qualify as a Cost and Management Accountant. Of all the departments I experienced, the one which I found the most interesting was Export Credit Control. I was fascinated by all the variations of trading terms, payment terms, marketing strategies and customer communications. I learned at an early stage that "one size fits all" cannot be applied to such a large variety of countries, markets and cultures.

My training as an accountant made me very comfortable with figures, which came in handy when negotiating with large-scale pan-European buyers and global manufacturers. Being able to understand balance sheets was also useful, as was my ability to differentiate between cost and perceived value.

When I joined Hotpoint, the company was part of the vast GEC group (with Lord Weinstock in charge) but in later years it was jointly owned 50:50 by GEC and the American giant, General Electric (led by Jack Welch). Witnessing the very different management styles of these two groups was wonderful experience for me, as was my involvement in Hotpoint's success. Hotpoint did not make the best domestic appliances in the market (as the Germans will tell you) but their marketing and their attention to the customer experience were outstanding. As a result, Hotpoint secured a very large share of the British market. In later years, I was able to share those best practices with collaborative manufacturers in other countries.

In September 1984, after fourteen years with Hotpoint, I became Export Manager, inheriting a piece of business worth two million pounds per annum. Progress was slow to begin with, but things changed when I had a new boss, Graham White – a fellow rock fan and fellow cricket fan. Graham provided the encouragement and support which Hotpoint's export efforts had not seen for many years. As a result, the annual exports grew to over sixteen million pounds by 1990.

I got a speaking date for Graham once, all about the forthcoming single European market, to a group of eminent Thessaloniki business people. The night before flying, I asked Graham how he would be travelling and he replied "pretty casual, you know – jeans". The following morning, I turned up at the airport in blue denim jeans, a black Hawkwind tee shirt and trainers. Graham appeared in a blazer, white shirt, silk tie, shiny black shoes and immaculately-pressed beige "jeans". By comparison, I looked more like his roadie.

One of my responsibilities was working with our American parent company to enable them to sell our products around the world under the General Electric brand. I found this work to be hugely enjoyable, but very challenging – GE had their pick of graduates from the Harvard Business School and some of them would be sent over to Europe to cut their teeth on us! The positive attitude in GE was so refreshing. If you made a mistake the reaction was always "what have you learned from that, buddy?" I developed enormously from that experience.

Talking of GE, I applied for a job once at GE's appliance head office in Louisville, Kentucky, and I was interviewed by the then VP of the appliances division, Jeff Immelt. Afterwards, Jeff phoned my boss to confirm that I had a good chance of getting the job. But then Jeff moved over to a different division in GE and his successor did away with the job for which I had applied. Jeff eventually succeeded Jack Welch as CEO and became one of America's most influential business leaders. No doubt he remembers me!

By the end of 2003, GEC's share of the company had been acquired by the Italian company, Merloni. I am afraid my punctuality and meticulous planning were not consistent with the Italian way of working, and I had reached the stage where I wasn't learning as much as I had been doing, so a very amicable parting of the ways was agreed. I had moved from Apprentice to Director in my time with Hotpoint, which looked good on the CV. My 33 years with the company, visiting 46 different countries and getting exposed to a number of business cultures, had been great experience and had mostly been good fun – but then it became time to apply that experience to other businesses, especially new exporters.

The second phase of my exporting career began at the beginning of 2004, when I started my own export consultancy business, Exportential Ltd. I delivered training courses, mentoring programmes and consultancy projects – sometimes delivering on behalf of other organisations and often collaborating with providers of complementary services. Most of this was within the East Midlands, but occasionally I got to work with businesses in places like Kent, Essex and Staffordshire.

Applying my big company experience to small businesses was challenging but very heartening when I saw rookie non-exporters become serious exporters in a number of markets. I reckon that I worked with about 500 small exporters over 19 years as a consultant, basically teaching them how to avoid the various pitfalls which I had experienced.

This is a "warts and all" work which is designed to supplement official export training courses, full of practical tips which are illustrated with real examples where appropriate. It is aimed at new exporters but I hope that there is enough general interest to appeal to people with no current exporting aspirations. As you will see from these pages, exporting can be tiring and frustrating – but, with plenty of preparation, it can be an enjoyable and profitable experience.

So, why am I qualified to write this? Because I have 38 years of exporting experience and I have committed or seen every mistake in the book!

# BREXIT

The final stage of my export consultancy career included **"Brexit"**. I recognised nine or ten months before the U.K. left the EU that there was no single reference point in my region on all things "Brexit", so I re-invented myself as that person. I attended numerous webinars and read profusely in order to get myself up to speed, including topics of which I had little prior knowledge. As a result, the period before and after the U.K. left the EU became the busiest and most lucrative of my working life. It was a very fitting swansong and I believe I made a real difference, ensuring that small traders coped with the various changes resulting from the U.K's exit from the EU.

I do not wish to make any political points about the U.K's decision to leave the EU. But I am a great supporter of the democratic process and I respected the outcome of the vote, so I supported its implementation. Too many people sat around after Brexit, saying "woe is me, I never voted for this". I encouraged them to stop feeling sorry for themselves and to make the best of the new circumstances. I got them to adopt a three point plan:-

1. Understand what the new rules are, especially in the areas of Incoterms, Rules Of Origin and VAT.
2. Understand what you have to do in order to comply with the new rules
3. Do whatever you have to do in order to minimise the effect on your customers, even if that means taking a short-term margin hit

Those exporters who failed to protect their EU customers from the effect of Brexit ended up losing those customers, and it is very difficult to win back customers who feel they have been neglected. I believe that looking after your customers and helping them through any period of change is important. Brexit was a very good example of this. Anyway, if you hear folks saying that Brexit brought no benefit for anyone, just ask my bank manager!

## DIANA

I joined Hotpoint at their factory in Llandudno Junction, North Wales, but it was made clear that, after my first sandwich course release, my future would be at their head office in Peterborough. It was there that I met the most significant person in my life, the person who would carry out the lion's share of parenting while I was away in airport departure lounges and the person who would support me after I started my own business.

Diana and I got engaged only ten weeks after our first date and we have been married since 1975. My exporting and consultancy careers couldn't have happened without Diana's understanding, patience and encouragement. And yet she has probably only ever been rewarded by receiving three "perks" from my various overseas contacts.

When my Maltese distributor's daughter got married, we were invited to attend the wedding and had the pleasure of staying at the Malta Hilton while we were over there. The experience was hampered a little by the fact that Diana was in the very early stages of pregnancy with our second daughter. But she got to witness the excellent Maltese hospitality at Valletta's wedding of the year.

I organised a distributor conference in Paris and the people helping me with hospitality told the owners of a Parisian restaurant, "Le Procope", that I was the decision maker and that I would be in Paris on a short break with my wife a couple of months before the conference. "Le Procope" claimed to be the oldest café in Paris and featured the original desk of Voltaire. The French onion soup was outstanding, as was the champagne cassis. Diana and I couldn't have been looked after any better by the team at "Le Procope" if we had been visiting royalty!

Mentioning royalty, brings me to Diana's third perk. One of the ladies working for my Irish distributor had a daughter who worked for U2's manager. I asked if she could get tickets for us to see U2 at Wembley Stadium and she arranged this for us. When turning up, we were ushered away from the normal entrances and over to the V.I.P. entrance. Diana then got to see her favourite band, U2, from the comfort of the Royal Box, alongside the band's friends and families!

Of course, she received perfume, chocolates and other duty-free gifts over the years. But I still owe her big time!

**EVANS**

A number of the anecdotes included in this book mention a character called "Evans", with whom I shared success, failure, happiness and much embarrassment.

Like myself, Stuart Evans was a proud Welshman. I would tease him that he came from the dirty, dusty part of Wales, whereas he claimed that I came from "Scouse Wales". We occasionally watched Welsh rugby matches on TV in foreign hotels and bars, accompanied by the local beverage. He spoke French very well and would often tease our colleagues with false information like "*coup de grace* is French for lawnmower" and "*cul de sac* is French for dismissal".

He was very handy in French restaurants because he knew what to order. However, we rarely broke the bank as we usually had Salade du Chef, lots of bread and red wine. One morning, when checking out from our hotel, he told me that he caught a dodgy late night film on one of the local French TV channels and his takeaway was "I'll never eat yoghurt again".

Stuart was bitten on the eyelid one night in Portugal and emerged from the hotel as though he had fought twelve rounds with Mike Tyson. I regret to admit that I thought he looked hilarious. His eyes were also the cause of a funny story which he told me. He and his wife had a tiff in their hotel room in France (or was it Corsica?) and she thumped him, giving him a black eye. He retaliated by saying "you dare do that again" – so she did. He then sat in the breakfast room the following morning like a bearded panda, with two black eyes, and embarrassingly came face to face with one of our biggest French customer's buyers!

Evans and I attended the christening of our Greek distributor's baby daughter. Being British, we turned up long before the Greek guests and we had time to kill. I stayed put while Stuart went off exploring – and he came back with dry cement from his foot to his knee. By then, other guests had arrived and they "helped" him by turning a tap on his white lower leg. From the christening we departed for a trade show and my super-professional colleague was dressed in an immaculate grey suit with one off-white leg, one black shoe and one white shoe.

Stuart could be infuriating when giving margin away, nearly always going just that bit too far below the "rock bottom" price. He could also be over-generous when giving money away for promotional support or exhibition support. But he was the most enthusiastic and effective colleague to have around at trade shows, which can be very arduous affairs.

Outside of work, Stuart and his wife, Pat, were wonderful hosts. Their Father's Day barbecue lunches were legendary. Pat has agreed with me that Stuart could delight and frustrate in equal measure. He was a good friend and the rascal has been greatly missed since his early death at the age of fifty eight.

# 1. WHY DO YOU WANT TO EXPORT?

The toughest thing about success is that you've got to keep on being a success (Irving Berlin)

Money is a good thing to have because it frees you from doing things you don't like. And since I dislike doing nearly everything, money is handy (Groucho Marx)

It has been said that arguing against globalisation is like arguing against the laws of gravity (Kofi Annan)

We will spend a great deal of time in this book looking at when and how you should export but, before we do that, it is necessary to step back and identify exactly WHY you want to export. Later thoughts on pricing and promotional activity will be heavily influenced by the reason why you are doing it – so it is important that you identify WHY you want to export, and then share that reason with your team.

Some years ago, a publication called "Export Times" surveyed their readership to find out the most common reason for starting down the export route – the most common was "because the boss thinks it would be a good idea". Rather than just guessing, I like to think that their bosses had thought things through and decided to proceed because of one of the following reasons.

### *Little Scope For Domestic Growth*

You can reach a stage whereby you have a good share of your domestic market but there is little scope for growth. Maybe you can grow that share by constantly coming up with ways of out-performing your competitors (this can be challenging), ways of innovative marketing (this can also be challenging) or under-cutting your competitors' prices. The last of these is a dangerous route to take, as you erode your margins, perhaps forever. So, the answer might be to robustly defend your domestic market share whilst pursuing export opportunities.

This may sound strange coming from an export promoter, but I try to get all prospective exporters to see if they can profitably increase their domestic activity before they dive into exporting. If they have explored all profitable domestic options, only then does it make sense to explore internationally.

### Excess Capacity

Throughout this book I refer to "products", but I include "services" in that description. So, when I say that excess capacity can cause a business to look for export opportunities, that can mean not just factory space or production lines, but also designers' time or programmers' time.

Where demand for a product is pretty even throughout the year, there may be an absolute excess in capacity. But what affects most businesses is the seasonality of demand, which means they are working every minute available at the height of the season yet struggling to fill their time in the "off" season. A solution here can be to find foreign markets where demand is either undeveloped or it peaks at those times of the year when domestic demand is low.

I must confess that I failed to address the seasonality of Hotpoint's business. The demand for things like fridges and tumble dryers is very seasonal but most of my sales were to Northern Hemisphere countries with the same seasons as ourselves. Doing export business during your domestic market's down period is very attractive, but far from easy. There is only so much you can sell to Chile!

### Vulnerability

A business which has all of its commercial activity in one domestic market can really be caught out if their only market suffers a slump. It is a case of "all your eggs in one basket" and you suffer, not from having done something wrong, it is just that there is a smaller pie to carve up.

By moving into export markets, you are effectively spreading your risks and making yourself less vulnerable. You will not be so affected by domestic market depressions when you have other activity in markets with different climates, geography, currencies or levels of affluence.

## *Experience for Business and Staff*

By becoming exposed to export markets, different negotiating techniques, innovative marketing tools and new business cultures, the business itself can become more rounded, as can the people who work in the business.

I once worked with a young export clerk whose inexperience of foreign matters led to her filing some correspondence from the Faeroes under "Egypt".

My Belgian distributor used to host a three day trade show, to which all trade customers and overseas suppliers were invited. At the end of the second day, all the overseas suppliers were invited to join the distributor's staff for a fine dinner. One of the suppliers, in an attempt to befriend the host, said "I am so pleased that you speak such good English, because I do not speak Belgian". Apart from the ignorance of not knowing they speak Flemish and French in Belgium, he clearly hadn't researched before travelling out there.

Travelling on export business can often expand your knowledge of other cultures, creeds and religions. When travelling through the Netherlands, I was once taken off the main road so I could see how the traditional Calvinist inhabitants of Staphorst lived, dressed and travelled.

## *Prestige and Morale*

There is no doubt that export success can have a very positive effect on a business, its staff, its suppliers and the local community. Maybe the local press can be persuaded to come and photograph a first shipment leaving for a new market, with the staff waving appropriate flags. The visit by a new export customer can create lots of local excitement and there are plenty of ways to give such a visit a high profile, without costing too much.

I always believed in sharing the details of export successes with all the people who had helped – like design engineers, production foremen, warehouse staff and printers. I once worked with a Sikh-owned business in Leicester which had picked up an impressive new order from Eastern Europe. I suggested that they make a big fuss for their staff but they refused because "if we tell them, they will just want more money!"

## *Merger & Acquisition*

Sometimes a business can find itself involved with international business as the result of having gone through a merger or an acquisition.

If your business has been bought by a parent company, sometimes the parent will bring to the party a ready-made network of overseas trading partners. Similarly, if your business acquires a foreign subsidiary, you may find that they have established distribution in new markets for you.

## *Obsolescence*

In the event of one of your products becoming obsolete, out of fashion or behind the times, it does not necessarily follow that they will be classed in a similar vein in less-sophisticated markets. As products move towards the latter stages of their life cycle, it makes absolute sense to look for overseas opportunities, where you can carry on supplying products long after their demise in the domestic market.

Alternatively, there are sometimes opportunities to export production line equipment and tooling to overseas countries, to enable local producers to carry on making your old products. And, of course, the people buying this equipment do not need to make the same marketing mistakes you may have made.

### *Economies Of Scale*

By venturing into export markets, and increasing the overall size of the business, you can take advantage of the resultant economies of scale. For instance, if you currently buy 100 components a year for your domestic production but then need to buy 120 a year to support your new export-boosted business, you can go back to your supplier and negotiate a better buying price – not just on the incremental volume, but on the whole purchase of 120. The new export volumes therefore can indirectly help to make your domestic sales more profitable.

When I visited Shanghai, I was very impressed at the sheer volume of street-based entrepreneurs they had and I was amused to hear a street vendor offering "umbrellas ten dollars each or two for 25 dollars". Not quite the point I was making!

### *Best Practices*

Visiting export markets enables you to pick up ideas which you can subsequently use in your domestic market. When I travelled abroad, I was constantly being asked what overseas market players were doing better than us. Were they introducing new features and benefits? Were they displaying products more imaginatively? Were they using innovative promotional tools?
Occasionally I would pick something up which my home market colleagues could modify and apply the idea locally. Graham White always argued that "nobody has a monopoly of wisdom" and it is surprising what you can achieve by

modifying someone else's idea – without stealing registered intellectual property, of course.

## *Don't Forget Why*

It is important to identify why you want to export, it is important to share the reason with your team, and it is important not to forget why you are doing it.

If your objective is to establish your brand in overseas markets, positioned similarly to the domestic market, then you will make more long-term decisions and you will invest more in the activity. However, if you are merely trying to shift your excess production, perhaps even using someone else's brand name, then you should not be committing too much time and money to the exercise.

In order to cope with additional turnover, sometimes you will have to invest in capital expenditure (machines, buildings, systems etc). Before committing to any such expenditure, you must ask the question "why" again. Perhaps, to avoid capital expenditure outlays, you could sub-contract things to other businesses, at least until you are more confident of the sustainability of the volumes.

So, down the road, when you are considering investment in styling, packaging or advertising – just stand back and ask yourself "why are we doing this?" The four Ps of marketing apply just as much to exporting and those four elements are all affected by the fundamental reason for starting.

# 2. ARE YOU READY TO EXPORT?

There is a danger in being persuaded before one understands (Woodrow Wilson)

To me, it is simple – if you are going to be thinking anyway, you might as well think big (Donald Trump)

If I had asked people what they wanted, they'd have said "faster horses" (Henry Ford)

As a promoter of exports, of course I encourage potential exporters to proactively seek overseas opportunities and contribute to our Balance of Payments. But only after I have satisfied myself that they are ready and fully prepared. If businesses dive into export markets before they have fully prepared themselves, they can experience great disappointment and lose money. They can end up in the wrong markets, with the wrong representatives and with inappropriate product offerings.

During my initial conversations with would-be exporters, I have adopted the role of devil's advocate, in order to ask searching and blunt questions, all designed to establish what has to be done in order to be ready.

### *Product Modifications*

One of the first things I learned as an exporter was that one size definitely does not fit all! For your standard product (or service of course) to be acceptable, attractive or desirable in another market, you will almost certainly have to carry out product modifications – some of which could be quite expensive. In some cases you will have to produce different items for different markets, but in other cases you will be able to modify your standard product so that it is acceptable in both domestic and export markets. Here are some of the reasons why your products may have to modified.

**Regulation and Compliance** – in some markets you will not be allowed to sell your products unless you acquire local approvals. Complying with the local test house or approvals body may necessitate subtle changes and, in some countries, this process can be painfully slow.

**Size** – the dimensions of your product may not be appropriate for other markets, often because of their need to be compatible with other things – housing units, doorways, railway gauges, carrying cases etc. And there are subtle differences between markets using metric dimensions and those using imperial dimensions (like the U.S.A.).

I was involved in the launch of new 2 metre high fridge freezers, with "childproof" controls which were situated at the very top of the appliance. The presentations in London, Paris and Dubai went very well but then disaster occurred in Tokyo. I was told "Mr Stokes, Japanese ladies cannot reach the controls". Back to the drawing board!

**Shape and Style** – fashions and consumer habits change, so you should be prepared to make amendments in order to avoid falling behind. However, you may be able to supply foreign markets with something they have not seen before. It can be a bold step to introduce new products into markets, so this should be done on the basis that you have something new and different to offer – and not to tell the locals that they are wrong.

The first time I went to South Korea, I suggested to my local representative that there appeared to be little chance of introducing our double-cavity cookers and front-loading washing machines into the market. I was wrong and my distributor was right – my next visit saw the leading retailer in Seoul prominently displaying both of those products.

**Colour** – do not underestimate the importance of colour in other markets, as this is not just a matter of fashion. Some colours have great significance due to traditional or religious reasons and must be respected. This can apply to your packaging as well as to your products, so this needs careful research before diving in.

Back in the 1980s, my colleagues made over 1000 washing machines in avocado green for the Iraqi market. Green is a significant colour in the Muslim world (look at their flags) and we were happy to comply with our customer's request.

**Language** – one of the biggest differences between ourselves and the rest of the world is that we speak different languages, and this is a major consideration when exporting. Printed text often appears on products, instruction books, packaging and labels. Supplying standard products in your language is arrogant and suggests that you have done little to recognise the needs of your export customers. You basically have three choices – (a) just supply your standard product, (b) make use of symbols instead of text, either for export-only items or for all items, and (c) supply specific export products, perhaps even for each individual market.

I always worked on the basis that if it is right to tell the customer something in their own language in your domestic market, then the export customer should be shown the same courtesy.

**Climate** – the performance and durability of products, packaging and labelling can be affected by the climatic conditions in your target market. And, of course, the climate can often determine from the outset that the demand for your product will be low – raincoats in Chad or sun cream in Iceland for instance. You will need to understand what happens to your product when it is used in, or exposed to, extremes of weather. Will it freeze, will it melt, will it get soggy? You may have to use alternative types of packaging to ensure your products arrive safely and without deterioration.

**Culture and Religion** – one of the biggest mistakes you can make in exporting is in failing to research the culture and religion in your target market. Local customs and practices may necessitate a re-design of your product, maybe even a name change to avoid any offence. You must check that any names, symbols, colours or slogans are acceptable in your target markets. There have been some spectacular mistakes made over the years which have led to the withdrawal of products and marketing campaigns.

The Spanish car manufacturer, Seat, had to change the name of their "Malaga" model for the Greek market, as "Malaga" sounds very much like the local Greek word for "wanker". In fact, it seems to be the most commonly-used word by Athenian taxi drivers!

Some years ago, GEC and Plessey merged their telecoms businesses and called the new business GPT – which proved to be embarrassing in France. GPT was pronounced "gee pee tee" in English but it was pronounced "jay pay tay" in French. This sounded like "j'ai pété" which means "I have farted".

**Packaging and Labelling** – you may have to change or "beef up" your packaging, depending upon

- The distance it will travel
- The time taken before reaching the customer
- The method of transport (German rail specifications can make compliance quite onerous)
- The conditions endured during the journey
- Methods of loading and unloading (clamp trucks, fork-lift trucks, cranes etc)

Similarly, you may well have to affix more or different labels to your products and you need to understand how complicated this will be before you start thinking about costs and pricing.

**Transferability of USPs** – your success in your domestic market will be due in no small part to the way you have exploited your Unique Selling Propositions (USPs). You need to think whether any necessary product modifications will dilute these USPs in any way. And are your USPs still valid in a new market with different competitive offerings? Just think realistically about whether your British USP is still valid once you have crossed the Channel.

Depending upon what local people think about Britain and its people, you may be able to use your Britishness as one of your USPs. If British quality, tradition and reputation are regarded favourably, then use them when selling in your target export markets.

**Intellectual Property** – protection of your Intellectual Property in overseas markets needs to be considered early on. Understand if you can register your trademarks in your target market and understand also if any patents you possess are applicable in your target market.

I remember a frustrated exporter to China telling me that protecting a trademark in that part of the world is a bit like the "Whack A Mole" game played in amusement arcades – as soon as you stop one culprit, up jumps another!

You may already have decided to use different brand names or sub-brand names because of pronunciation, religious offence or local meanings. But, whatever names you choose to use, check early on if you are <u>allowed</u> to use them. Just because you have an established website, it doesn't follow that you will obtain an overseas trademark.

**Late Point Differentiation** – whenever you have to make a different product for an export market, it is sensible to make any necessary changes as late in the production process as possible. So, send domestic and export products down the same route for as long as possible, before differentiating them at the end.

## *Capacity*

Before embarking upon an export journey, a business needs to establish whether it has the capacity to cope with the increased demand which will come from new markets. It is pointless spending much time on identifying markets and finding representatives if you are then unable to supply your new-found buddies. I believe that there are four areas where you can be caught out.

**Physical Equipment** – what spare capacity do you have now and, more importantly, what spare capacity do you have at the busiest time of the year? Suppose your export adventures result in a 20% increase in sales – how are you going to support that? If you are clever, or lucky, your export sales will be achieved during your domestic "off" season – but if export demand mirrors domestic demand, you need to have an overtime strategy in place (which will affect the cost of the product of course). We are talking not just of production line capacity, but also of machine shop capacity, tooling limits and specialist equipment (finishing, packaging, labelling etc). It is important that you identify any potential bottlenecks early in the piece.

**Human Resources** – sometimes your product does not consist of physical items but things like software, consultancy, animation or music. Here, the important constraint is the human beings who compose, invent, develop and finish the product. Again, seasonality has to be considered.

You will also have to consider whether you have enough sales staff, admin staff, warehousing personnel and credit controllers. Perhaps you could positively discriminate in favour of linguists when recruiting new members of staff – because no-one speaks your language when you are chasing payments!

**Systems** – you need to consider whether your manual and digital systems are sufficiently robust to handle more products, material requisitions, orders, invoices and payments. New systems may have to be installed and staff will have to be trained in how to use them.

**Suppliers** – this is always the one that catches people out. If you are likely to increase your activity because of export initiatives, then someone needs to share that information with the business' critical suppliers. What seasonal pressures do your suppliers have? What tooling constraints might hinder their supplies to you? You need to keep close to your suppliers to ensure they can grow with you.

*People*

As well as considering how much spare capacity your people have (especially creative people like designers, programmers etc) you will need to think closely about:-

- What training will need to be provided and who will be able to provide it?
- What new systems and procedures will be necessary and how much will they cost?
- Perhaps most importantly – who will cover for the person who will be leading the export initiative? If the MD will be taking the lead, then while the MD is abroad, who will do the things the MD normally does? If you do not give serious consideration to "who covers for the MD", I guarantee that as soon as

29

the next domestic market crisis occurs, the new export plans will be neglected or shelved.

## *Finance*

When embarking upon an export strategy, there is no escaping the fact that the business will incur additional costs – some predictable and some not. This is not an exhaustive list, but it includes some of the additional costs encountered by new exporters:-

- Product modifications
- Additional kit or machines
- New systems or software
- Website modifications
- New brochures
- Translation costs
- Travel costs
- Business insurance (especially if you plan to supply North America)
- Intellectual property costs
- Credit insurance premiums

These are definitely not reasons for turning your back on exporting but they need to be identified and budgeted before you proceed. You need to walk into exporting with both eyes open if you are to achieve profitable, sustainable business.

# 3. HOW DO YOU GET STARTED IN EXPORT?

Consultants are people who borrow your watch, tell you what time it is, and then walk off with your watch (Robert Townsend)

Take risks. If you win, you will be happy – if you lose, you will be wise (Anon)

Business opportunities are like buses, there is always another one coming along (Richard Branson)

So far we have established your reason for exporting and confirmed that you are ready to export. So, how do you actually make a start? This is the step-by-step approach needed:-

- **Establish why you want to export** and share the reasons with your team (chapter 1 examined this in some depth).
- **Confirm that you are ready to start exporting** (chapter 2 looked at the various things to put in place)
- **Identify your initial target markets** (chapter 4 will explain how to do this).
- **Identify the most appropriate routes to market** (chapter 5 will explore the alternatives).
- **Really commit some time to researching your target markets** and the potential trading partners. This will include desk research, purchased data, use of a third party (consultant, Chamber of Commerce, Government departments) and your own market visits. The only way to understand a market is to visit the place yourself and, as well as picking up lots of information about your new market, you will also learn a lot about the people, the culture and the way they live their lives. I must stress that I was not paid to be a tourist but occasionally I had spare time (between meetings, if I had arrived early for a meeting due to flight availability, cancelled meetings etc) to look around places.
  On my first visit to Istanbul, I was surprised to find, not a local musical offering, but a Canadian blues duo entertaining the hotel guests. I wasn't expecting the songs of Robert Johnson to be heard drifting over the Bosphorus!

During a visit to Helsinki, I unexpectedly came across an Irish poet in a bar, reciting the material he had written – and it was in English, not Finnish.

On other visits I was lucky enough to catch football games in Madrid (the Bernabeu Stadium was awesome), Bilbao, Thessaloniki and Dublin. I learned that Spanish fans were very respectful towards match officials but the Greeks almost lynched a poor old linesman!

One evening, I was taken to a Basque men-only gastronomic club in Bilbao where the members actually prepared and cooked the food. As the guest of honour I was looked after regally, with plenty of top quality Rioja.

I had the pleasure of several journeys by Shinkansen (the Japanese "bullet trains") and I noticed they had areas at the end of each carriage for the use of mobile phones, thus ensuring that other travellers were not disturbed. What a pity the U.K. cannot do something similar.

- **Select your partner or representative** in your target market (chapter 6 covers this in detail).
- **Agree brand and product launch activities** with your new representative. These may include press releases, trade shows, exhibitions, conferences, literature, trade press ads, radio ads, trade or consumer offers, sales training support and technical training support.
- **Drive the relationship**, as covered in chapter 13. The signing up of a new representative is the beginning, not the end, of the hard work. It is vital that you take the lead and do not leave everything to your new partner – establish from the outset that the tail will not wag the dog! This will involve you in regular visits to

the market to ensure that your representative is handling your affairs in the way in which you want. On one occasion I visited my Belgian distributor during a football World Cup tournament and I was invited to join a group of Antwerp dignitaries to watch on a large screen a needle match between Belgium and the Netherlands. The match ended goalless, but not without incident. The evening was quite raucous, especially after several Duval beers! On a trip to Shanghai, I was invited to a place acting as a workshop, museum and (of course) sales office for local pearls. Our guide was a very attractive and elegantly-dressed young lady who ended her presentation by calmly walking over to a large spittoon, into which she spectacularly cleared her throat!

- **Do not lose sight of the 4 Ps**, or the way they are bound together by the fifth P. Preparing your entry into a new export market is no different to any other marketing exercise – you need to understand your four Ps and how to bind them together.

  *Product* – the actual product, or service, that you will present to the market, and the brands you will use

  *Price* – the price you will charge and the margins available to everyone in the chain

  *Place* – the geographical area covered and the routes to market you will use

  *Promotion* – the marketing tools you will use to attract end users as well as trade customers. This could include online and physical material, depending upon the product or service being offered.

Having recognised what your four Ps are, it is vital that all four are positioned <u>consistently</u>. You cannot offer high quality products at dirt cheap prices. You cannot advertise your products in top quality magazines and then sell them through budget-end retailers. And, of course, it does not make sense to offer up-market items to markets where disposable income is low. Failing to position your four Ps consistently will mean your performance is poor or even non-existent.

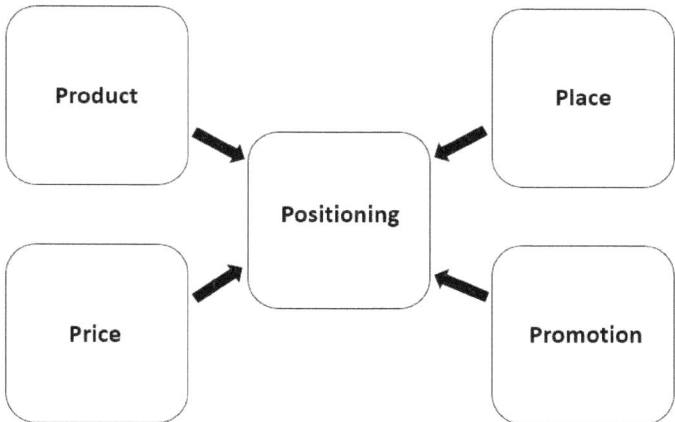

Just grade your four Ps as "Top, Middle or Bottom". The answer needs to be the same for all four.

# 4. WHERE WILL YOU START?

Never look down to test the ground before taking your next step. Only he who keeps his eye fixed on the far horizon will find his right road. (Dag Hammarskjöld)

Discovery consists not in seeking new landscapes but in having new eyes. (Marcel Proust)

The man who stops advertising to save money is like the man who stops the clock to save time. (Anon)

You simply cannot spread yourself too thinly by going after too many markets at once. You should concentrate on being excellent in a small number of markets initially. I recommend that new exporters start with no more than one or two target markets. You will have seen business people who have large world maps on the wall behind them, decorated by pins denoting overseas representatives. It is not the number of pins which is important, it is the value of business each one generates. Don't be a pin pusher!

When deciding which export markets you will target, it is important to plot a graph, showing the **Size Of Opportunity** against the **Ease Of Access**.

The Size Of Opportunity should be a weighted average of Population Size, Population Growth, Population Demographics, GDP and Climate. There could of course also be sector-specific factors which will significantly affect the weighted average.

Some years ago I was looking at potential new markets for a range of storage heaters which operated by building up heat during the "white meter" hours and releasing the heat during the daytime. If a country did not have an off-peak electricity rate, then they were not a market for our heaters. This limited us to about 12 countries around the world but it was the single most important factor. Thankfully one of the countries was Finland, which was an excellent place to visit and to do business. Another was New Zealand, where our main contact was a lady named Rosie Hosie – honestly!

Ease Of Access should be a weighted average of Import Controls, Trade Agreements, Intellectual Property, Proximity, Language and Business Culture.

So, you are plotting the actual and potential volume against the barriers or difficulties you may face. In some cases, this exercise can be completed fairly quickly but be prepared for it lasting a while. It is important that you get it right, so do not rush things. Some of the research to get the numbers you need can be done by your own team of people, or you can use intermediaries (students, market research consultants, Government departments etc). Try to confirm any data by using more than one source and be prepared to pay for good quality data.

The resultant Market Selection graph will look like this:-

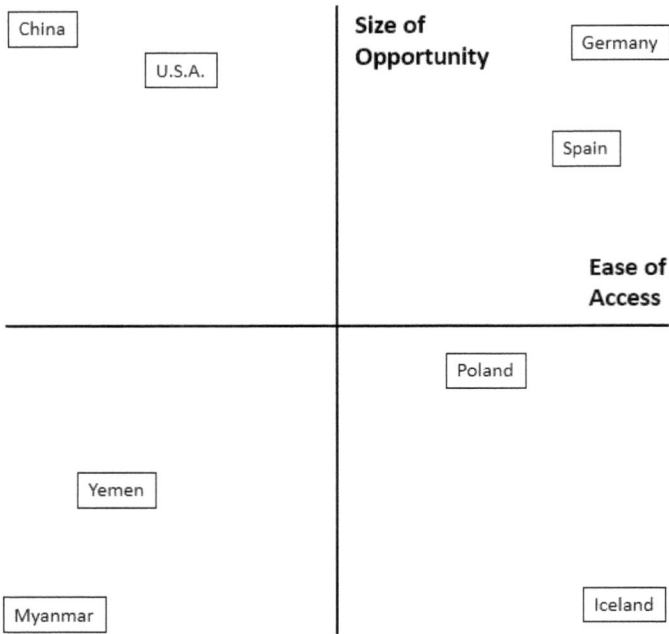

In this example, the obvious targets would be those at the top right of the graph. They offer a decent-sized opportunity, without being very difficult to access (Germany followed by Spain in this case).

Difficult markets offering a low opportunity (bottom left of the graph) should simply be ignored, as your time can be far better utilised elsewhere.

The tricky decision comes when you have to compare High Opportunity, Difficult to Enter markets (China and U.S.A. in the example) and those which are Smaller Opportunities but relatively Easy To Enter (Poland and Iceland).

Occasionally, you will get lucky. You will spot an opportunity which is simply too good to miss. I was involved in exporting at the time when the U.K. still had a lot of military personnel stationed in Germany. These soldiers and RAF people had their families with them and much of their shopping was done with the U.K. forces retail organisation, NAAFI. Over the years, I visited most of NAAFI's stores in North Rhine Westphalia to maintain their support. The forces families were extremely patriotic, buying British goods wherever possible.

When conducting market research, you will learn a lot about business and personal etiquette in those markets. The more prepared you are, the better you will perform.

Early in my exporting career, I was eating a fish meal with a new contact in the Netherlands and I was determined to display good manners and not let myself down. Unfortunately, I squeezed the lemon too enthusiastically – straight in my eye. I spent the rest of the meal addressing my new Dutch friend with a decided twitch and a bloodshot eye.

I had two difficulties when I first visited Hong Kong. At my opening meal the actual food was positioned right in the middle of a large turntable. This was no problem for those who were adept with chopsticks – but I couldn't get anything over without dropping it. I didn't eat much that night!

That evening finished up with tequila slammers – a ritual whereby you drink a tequila straight down and then nominate the next person to do likewise. That was all very well, but the one person known to everyone else was me – so every second or third nomination was "Mike Stokes".

During a rare visit to Budapest, sales executives from my parent company, GEC, were meeting some senior officials in the Hungarian air force and they asked if I would attend, to fill out the numbers. The meal was held in a magnificent restaurant and the food was excellent. Unfortunately, the lady sitting next to me (the wife of one of the Hungarian officials) became more and more inebriated, and increasingly "friendly", as the evening wore on. I thought the taxis would never arrive!

Over dinner, my host in Lisbon, the charming Luis Dos Santos, kindly offered me a ticket to the 1997 Portuguese Cup Final between Benfica and Boavista – but that would have meant extending my visit by two more days, so I had to pass on that one.

Travelling to other markets is the only way in which you can fully understand local variations and nuances. And then you can begin to see how local practices affect customer expectations. Remember, if something is different from your UK experiences, it is just different – not wrong!

Some new exporters spread their risks by starting off with two quite different target markets. Maybe one will be a euro market and one will be linked to the US dollar. Perhaps one will be in the EU while one will be in the Middle East.

Later in his career, whilst with UKTI, Evans somehow got permission to take a party of Lincolnshire exporters to Burkina Faso. How that place ended up on anyone's "potential market" radar is beyond me but nonetheless Evans took his party out there – and then proceeded to lose one of the delegates. They eventually found him in the local jail, the result of a misunderstanding!

Transparency International is a global movement working in over 100 countries to end the injustice of corruption. Each year, Transparency International produces a **Corruption Perception Index** (CPI), which ranks 180 countries and territories around the world by their perceived levels of public sector corruption. This report is a very useful point of reference, especially if you plan to deal in a country, as opposed to dealing with a country. This chart should be referenced if you are setting up Franchising, Licensing or JV arrangements. New Zealand, Singapore and the Scandinavian countries regularly appear at the top of this list. Number 1 is perceived as the least corrupt and number 180 is perceived as the most corrupt.

# CORRUPTION PERCEPTION INDEX 2022

| | | | | | |
|---|---|---|---|---|---|
| 1 | Denmark | 61 | Jordan | 116 | Ukraine |
| 2 | Finland | 61 | Malaysia | 116 | Zambia |
| 2 | New Zealand | 63 | Armenia | 123 | Dominican Republic |
| 4 | Norway | 63 | Romania | 123 | Kenya |
| 5 | Singapore | 65 | China | 123 | Niger |
| 5 | Sweden | 65 | Cuba | 126 | Bolivia |
| 7 | Switzerland | 76 | Montenegro | 126 | Laos |
| 8 | Netherlands | 65 | Sao Tome and Principe | 126 | Mexico |
| 9 | Germany | 69 | Bahrain | 126 | Uzbekistan |
| 10 | Ireland | 69 | Jamaica | 130 | Djibouti |
| 10 | Luxembourg | 69 | Oman | 130 | Egypt |
| 12 | Hong Kong | 72 | Benin | 130 | Eswatini |
| 13 | Australia | 72 | Bulgaria | 130 | Mauritania |
| 14 | Canada | 72 | Ghana | 130 | Papua New Guinea |
| 14 | Estonia | 72 | Senegal | 130 | Togo |
| 14 | Iceland | 72 | South Africa | 136 | Gabon |
| 14 | Uruguay | 77 | Burkina Faso | 137 | Mali |
| 18 | Belgium | 77 | Hungary | 137 | Paraguay |
| 18 | Japan | 77 | Kuwait | 140 | Russia |
| 18 | United Kingdom | 77 | Solomon Islands | 140 | Kyrgyzstan |
| 21 | France | 77 | Timor-Leste | 140 | Pakistan |
| 22 | Austria | 7 | Trinidad and Tobago | 142 | Cameroon |
| 23 | Seychelles | 77 | Vietnam | 142 | Liberia |
| 24 | United States of America | 84 | Kosovo | 142 | Madagascar |
| 25 | Bhutan | 85 | Guyana | 142 | Mozambique |
| 25 | Taiwan | 85 | India | 142 | Uganda |
| 27 | Chile | 85 | Maldives | 147 | Bangladesh |
| 27 | United Arab Emirates | 85 | North Macedonia | 147 | Guinea |
| 29 | Barbados | 85 | Suriname | 147 | Iran |
| 30 | Bahamas | 85 | Tunisia | 150 | Afghanistan |
| 31 | Israel | 91 | Belarus | 150 | Cambodia |
| 31 | South Korea | 91 | Colombia | 150 | Central African Republic |
| 33 | Lithuania | 91 | Moldova | 150 | Guatemala |
| 33 | Portugal | 94 | Argentina | 150 | Lebanon |
| 35 | Botswana | 94 | Brazil | 150 | Nigeria |
| 35 | Cabo Verde | 94 | Ethiopia | 150 | Tajikistan |
| 35 | St Vincent & the Grenadines | 94 | Morocco | 157 | Azerbaijan |
| 35 | Spain | 94 | Tanzania | 157 | Honduras |
| 39 | Latvia | 99 | Cote d'Ivoire | 157 | Iraq |
| 40 | Qatar | 99 | Lesotho | 157 | Myanmar |
| 41 | Czechia | 101 | Albania | 157 | Zimbabwe |
| 41 | Georgia | 101 | Ecuador | 162 | Eritrea |
| 41 | Italy | 101 | Kazakhstan | 162 | Sudan |
| 41 | Slovenia | 101 | Panama | 164 | Congo |
| 45 | Dominica | 101 | Peru | 164 | Guinea-Bissau |
| 45 | Poland | 101 | Serbia | 166 | Democratic Republic of the Congo |
| 45 | Saint Lucia | 101 | Sri Lanka | 167 | Chad |
| 48 | Costa Rica | 101 | Thailand | 167 | Comoros |
| 49 | Fiji | 101 | Turkey | 167 | Nicaragua |
| 49 | Slovakia | 110 | Bosnia and Herzegovina | 167 | Turkmenistan |
| 51 | Cyprus | 110 | Gambia | 171 | Burundi |
| 51 | Greece | 110 | Indonesia | 171 | Equatorial Guinea |
| 51 | Grenada | 110 | Malawi | 171 | Haiti |
| 54 | Malta | 110 | Nepal | 171 | North Korea |
| 54 | Rwanda | 110 | Sierra Leone | 171 | Libya |
| 54 | Saudi Arabia | 116 | Algeria | 176 | Yemen |
| 57 | Croatia | 116 | Angola | 177 | Venezuela |
| 57 | Mauritius | 116 | El Salvador | 178 | South Sudan |
| 59 | Namibia | 116 | Mongolia | 178 | Syria |
| 60 | Vanuatu | 116 | Philippines | 180 | Somalia |

Source : Transparency International

# 5. FINDING OVERSEAS TRADING PARTNERS

It is well known what a middleman is – he is someone who bamboozles one party and plunders the other. (Benjamin Disraeli)

Sell a man a fish, he eats for a day. Teach a man to fish, you ruin a wonderful business opportunity. (Karl Marx)

Number one, cash is king. Number two, communicate. Number three, buy or bury the competition. (Jack Welch)

If you are supplying a digital product or service – software, animation, music, online books etc – then you may well be able to handle export markets directly from your base in the U.K. But most exporters (even if you are selling to overseas customers via your website) will need a trading partner to help them in foreign markets. A number of factors will affect what type of trading partner you need – geographical size of market, proximity, likely scale of demand, culture, language and religion. Also, your decision will be influenced by the nature of your goods – are they purely bespoke, is there a long lead time, will you be required to provide comprehensive technical support?

**These are the main routes to market.**

**Direct** – if you have the resources to receive orders via your website, you can pack and dispatch your goods, you can provide a suitable customer information service and you have the wherewithal to manage your marketing in other markets, then you probably don't need overseas trading partners. You will still need to liaise closely with your chosen logistics provider, with HMRC and with your local Chamber of Commerce to ensure that you comply with all the necessary international trade regulations.

If you choose to deal on a direct basis with your consumers, you must give careful thought to the languages used on your website, the customer contact telephone numbers given out on your website and the linguistic abilities of whoever is answering those telephones.

Dealing direct sounds nice and simple but you must consider the customer experience. Are you easy to deal with? If you are confident that you can provide the same level of excellent service to your overseas customers as you do to your U.K. customers, then go direct. But if you can't do so, you should look at the other routes to market, using local partners where appropriate.

**Fulfilment House** – many exporters who sell through their own website, use the services of Fulfilment Houses to handle the customer-facing responsibilities. These organisations typically maintain local stocks, arrange for delivery to the customer, provide call centre facilities and possibly run a sales ledger as well. They do not take orders, they do not carry out negotiations on your behalf and they are not your representatives as such.

**Agent** – an agent represents the exporter and is authorised to conduct negotiations on your behalf. An agent will often collect orders for you but rarely receives customers' payments on your behalf. Agents usually have sales targets to achieve (not easy to set up in the early days) and they are rewarded with commissions. Agents do not carry stock and they have no direct transactional relationship with the customers. Their existence must be formalised by means of a Sales Agency Agreement. If you decide to appoint an agent in the EU, do not proceed on the basis of a handshake because under EU law, the default position is heavily weighted in favour of the agent.

**Distributor** – many exporters will refer to their overseas representatives as "agents" but what they actually have are distributors. If your representative buys products from you, stocks those products and then sells those products to customers, then your representative is a distributor and NOT an agent. Your distributor works in the local market very much as you do in the U.K. They will handle all the marketing, stocking, selling, delivering and (where appropriate) servicing of your products. You will negotiate their buying prices but you cannot dictate their selling prices.

And again, the relationship must be formalised by means of a Distributor Agreement.

In the case of digital products, distributors are often called "Resellers", with the same set of responsibilities.

**Franchising** – this is not the most common route into export markets but it works if you want a fairly hands on arrangement. The franchisee receives your permission to use your products, your brands and your processes. The franchisee sells the products and pays you an agreed percentage of the sales value. The franchisee is restricted as to the way in which the business is run, whilst the franchisor has responsibility for marketing, product development and training of the franchisee's staff. For franchising to work, the arrangement has to be sufficiently financially interesting for both parties. Respective responsibilities should be laid out in a Franchising Agreement. It is fundamentally important that you have your Intellectual Property in place before you start a conversation on Franchising. You should not talk about franchising your business until you have registered a trademark in the target country.

**Licensing** – this route is rarely used by new exporters but may be applied where an exporter recognises an opportunity but does not want to devote much time to it. It is also quite a common way of entering developing markets, where there is an outright ban upon the importation of your items. It involves the granting of permission to the licensee (often a manufacturer) to use your brand name in agreed territories and you receive royalty payments as a percentage of the licensee's sales value. A Licensing Agreement will cover which territories have been agreed and should also say something about preventing the licensee from supplying your home market or any other markets where you are active.

It is fundamentally important that you have your Intellectual Property in place before you start a conversation on Licensing. You should not license the use of your brand name if you have not registered a trademark in the target country.

**Joint Venture** – sometimes the only route for you in an export market (especially a developing market) is by setting up a Joint Venture. This is where two organisations (yourself and usually a business already established in the export market) set up a Joint Venture company, owned by both parties. It must be clearly indicated which organisation has management responsibility (nearly always the local business) and what the duties of each business entail.

In the mid 1990s, I was involved in a failed JV attempt in Ukraine. It failed because the two parties' objectives were dissimilar. We wanted something for nothing and they just wanted to be bought by a big western company. At the early stages of the negotiations, I was used on a fact-finding mission, accompanying the local sales manager around dealers and factory stores. At least I got to enhance my knowledge of the barter system!

In 2008, I was fortunate enough to take part in a market visit to China, with eleven other export advisers, organised by the China-Britain Business Council. We were discussing the various routes to market available and Joint Ventures were brought up. One of our Chinese hosts told us that "Joint Ventures are like two people sleeping in the same bed, but with different dreams".

**Merger** – one way of entering a new export market is to merge your business with a local business which is already established in the export market. Negotiations can take a long time, and your outlay can be substantial but it means that you hit the ground running by working with someone already active in your target market.

**Acquisition** – going one stage even further, the outright purchase of a local business will give you an instant presence in your target market but it obviously can cost a lot. Again, there will be plenty of negotiating involved, as you will be keen to hang on to the key individuals in the acquired business.

**Associate Business of Domestic Customer** – take a look at your customers in the U.K. and explore which of them has associations in foreign markets. Some of your customers may have parent companies based abroad, some of them may have sister companies abroad and some of them may be part of cross-border buying groups. Use these relationships to your advantage, but be careful not to compromise the existing U.K. situation by quoting "creative" export pricing. Your U.K. customers will be smart enough to spot opportunities too. They will want to help you but of course they will want to know what is in it for them.

**Overseas Branch or Subsidiary** – one route forward is to create a branch or subsidiary of your U.K. business. It is relatively simple to do, although you must take advice on the local legal requirements, financial responsibilities and Human Resource issues. This is not a particularly quick route to market, but it does give you control and it is certainly a positive statement about your commitment to the new market.

It is not necessary to use just one route to market in every country, or even in the same country. You could appoint a distributor to supply small retailers, whilst using an agent to secure full-container orders from large retailers.

Having established the most appropriate route to market for your target market, you now have to identify the likely profile of an ideal trading partner in that market. You will probably ask the following questions:-

- Where should they be located?
- What transport and storage facilities should they have?
- What sales force should they have?
- What back office facilities and systems should they have?
- How should they be handling after sales servicing?
- What types of other brand should they be carrying?
- How should their finances be looking?

**Research** – in order to make contact with your ideal trading partner, you will need to conduct lots of research. A mistake I have often seen from British exporters is the failure to do enough research. They dive in too soon and then they end up with the wrong representative, located in the wrong place and with a track record of working with unsuitable principals. Of course, you cannot just do research, eventually you have to make a decision. But it is essential that lots of hard work is done at the beginning, to prevent disappointment and disillusionment later on.

Options with regard to research include the following:-

*Own Staff* – if you have people who are "internet savvy", familiar with your products and comfortable with foreign languages, it makes sense to use them.

*Students* – your local university may well have resources amongst (a) British students studying international trade or (b) overseas students with language proficiency. The universities will probably charge for their services, but in my experience the amount will be far from prohibitive.

*Market Research Specialists* – there are many specialists out there who will conduct research on your behalf. Yes, they will be expensive but, if they are properly briefed, they can be excellent value. You need to decide whether or not you want such people to actually contact the prospective partners or not.

*Government Departments* – some British embassies and consulates offer a research facility to British exporters. This is chargeable but well worth exploring. They can, if instructed, contact local businesses on your behalf, to see if they might be interested in an exploratory meeting with you.

*Overseas Chambers of Commerce* – in some countries the local Chamber will help you to identify potential partners, as long as you clearly depict the kind of business you seek.

*Internet* – there is an awful lot you can pick up from the Internet, especially if you search for key words in the local language and via the local search engines. So, don't search for "agent", "distributor" or "reseller" – search for the local translations of those words. If you are looking for a representative in a particular sector, search for translated versions of the key products they might carry. There are often online lists of local trade associations' members, trade directories and business events.

*Trade Shows* – the effective use of overseas trade shows is covered in Chapter 10. Any data you pick up from other Internet searches can be corroborated by information gleaned from trade show websites – if businesses are as important and influential as they say they are, why are they not exhibiting at their sector's prime trade show?

Once you have established the most appropriate route to market, and identified some prospective trading partners, you need to evaluate one business against another. Once you have a short list of candidates, it may be necessary to conduct some more research before going ahead with the comparison.

# 6. EVALUATION AND COMPARISON OF POTENTIAL PARTNERS

The entrepreneur always searches for change, responds to it, and exploits it as an opportunity. (Peter Drucker)

A traveller without observation is a bird without wings. (Moslih Eddin Saadi)

If two men on the same job agree all the time, then one of them is useless. If they disagree all the time, then both are useless. (Darryl Zanuck)

When comparing the various overseas trading partners, you will need to consider the following areas:-

**Location** – it is important to consider where the candidates are based geographically. You need to satisfy yourself that such businesses can cover all of the area you want, especially those areas from which your likely sales will be achieved. In the case of most products or services, you will seek representatives who are best-equipped to serve the main areas of population. But this is not always the case. If the majority of your representative's sales are likely to be to farmers, for instance, then it would make more sense that they be located in a regional town or city, rather than the capital city. Some countries are simply too big to be handled by one agent or distributor and you should look to handle those markets via a number of regional specialists (China, India, U.S.A. are good examples). You should be wary of small businesses who claim to cover large markets on their own.

A potential Greek distributor was keen to show me how they could handle the whole country, especially the northern part – which had been under Turkish rule until 1912. Unfortunately, he got his terminology wrong as he tried to inform me that a number of his staff had mixed Greek and Turkish blood. "We are good bastards here", he told me.

**Experience** – although youthful enthusiasm is to be admired, you should be looking for people who know what they are doing. You are looking for people who will be your eyes and ears in the market, people who will know what to do when they are confronted by challenges. Your potential partners should be able to demonstrate an impressive track record with regard to representing foreign suppliers in their local market.

**Positioning** – it is important that you are represented by someone with experience of products whose positioning is similar to your own. If you are positioned "mid to high end" then you will struggle to progress with someone whose experience and expertise comes from operating with "budget" items. Sales forces whose mindset is "budget priced", very often fail to appreciate the principle of "selling up" through the range.

**Other Products Carried** – you will get a good idea of how a local representative conducts the business when you find out which other products and brands they carry. If they carry low-priced, low-quality items, this may not do you any favours, if your aspirations are for a "mid to high" level of market entry.

Over the years, you will recognise a number of brands which sit comfortably alongside your brand and by exploiting that relationship, you may be able to grow your distribution. I was fortunate enough over the years to work with people who also represented the likes of Kenwood (small appliances), Fisher (video and audio equipment) and Daikin (airconditioning).

**Influence in the Local Market** – once you have appointed your new trading partner, you will want to hit the ground running. You therefore need to seek evidence that they are known and have a good reputation in the market. Establish which distribution channels they are currently working with. Are they members of any local trade association or chamber of commerce? Do they speak at any sector-specific conferences or events?

**Financial Standing** – you need to satisfy yourself that any potential trading partner is sound financially, so do not be afraid to ask for the latest set of accounts. If they will be buying products from you, you need to know that they can pay you, so carry out whatever credit checks you think are appropriate. If you are unable to get credit insurance on a particular buyer, that may generate a few warning signs for you.

**Staff** – we looked earlier at the importance of location, but that is not so important if the business has sales (and perhaps sales support) staff spread across the territory. The capability of the business' sales team is vitally important, so don't be afraid to probe as to what experience they have, what they are selling now, and what they have sold before.
As well as understanding the sales capabilities, also try to understand who are the other key individuals in the business. When the boss is not around, who takes charge? Who are the people without whom they would struggle (maybe software designers, technical experts, marketing executives etc)?

**Resources** – depending upon your sector, you will expect to find certain resources within a well-established partner business. These might include:-
*Showroom*
*Office Premises*
*Meeting Rooms*
*Warehousing*
*Training Facilities*
*Vehicles (cars, vans, trucks, fork-lift or clamp trucks)*
*Specialist Equipment*
One distributor was keen to impress upon me that they inspect every one of their new products in great detail before going ahead. The intention was to show how detailed and meticulous they were. "Yes, Mr Stokes, we take all products and we striptease them so that we know them".

**Attitude** – the people with whom you choose to work must have the same mindset as yourself. They should be punctual (this can be a bit of a challenge in some countries), they should not be resistant to change, they should have a "can do" philosophy and they should ideally be brimming with ideas. When you have evaluated a number of potential candidates, you eventually get a "gut feel" about whether someone is right or not. When you enter a new market there will be any number of roadblocks and frustrations, so you must be happy that your chosen representative is a good fit. My best distributors were always the ones who were constantly pushing back at me with new ideas. I got frustrated by the ones who didn't come up with anything new, leaving everything to me.

**Language Issues** – it helps if you find out which English speakers are in the organisation – especially if you are chasing outstanding payments!

I was checking out a Spanish distributor alongside my American colleague from GE, Bob Ogburn. I asked Bob if he spoke any Spanish and he replied, "Hell, I thought I spoke English until I met you".

Although it is nice if your trading partners speak English, I learned over the years that local people will regard you as courteous if you can at least master 7 words, which I call *"The Magnificent Seven"*, in their language:-

1.  Hello
2.  Goodbye
3.  Yes
4.  No
5.  Please
6.  Thank You
7.  Cheers

Sometimes I would accidentally use my customers' versions instead of the correct ones. I found myself saying "approximatively" on occasions, as well as using "fifteen days" instead of "fortnight".

I spoke reasonable "schoolboy" French but I needed an interpreter to handle technical issues. On one occasion my interpreter (also the wife of my spare parts distributor) was late arriving in Paris from Rouen. I therefore had to start negotiating an After Sales Service Agreement with the pan-European retailer, Carrefour, all in French. I am proud to say that I managed 18 of the 20 points on my own, before my interpreter arrived to clear up the others.

**Volunteers** – so far, I have covered the scenario where you find a target market, conduct your research, identify potential representatives and then compare the candidates. This is undoubtedly the safest and most reliable way to proceed when entering new export markets. However, there are times when you will be contacted by overseas businesses, volunteering to represent you in their markets.

People find your details on websites, in online directories, at trade shows and via third party contacts. They read all about you and your products and then they approach you with enormous enthusiasm, offering to help you in their market. So, how should you react?

Well, when you take on a distributor, reseller or agent, one of the important things to do is to enthuse, energise and motivate your new partner. When you have a volunteer standing in front of you, then that job is not necessary – they are already enthused!

It is important to manage their expectations, without dampening their enthusiasm. They may well be based in one of those markets which were identified as "Small Opportunity" or "Difficult To Access". But just because they are very keen to proceed, you still need to evaluate them in the same way as you have done for other potential partners.

The conventional way is by far the more likely to work, but just occasionally one will drop in your lap when you least expect it. I never targeted Cyprus, Greece or the Czech Republic – but they all found me!

**Scams** – there was a time when overseas scams consisted of individuals pretending that the member of an African royal family had died and had left a sum of money to you. All you had to do was dial a number or send your bank details. They have moved on from there by pretending to be sourcing officials working on behalf of overseas Government departments or large corporations. They say that there is considerable interest in your products, but before placing an order for several thousand items, they just need you to send some free of charge samples.

Real businesses would not approach you like this, so you should respond by stating that all samples must be paid for, in advance of shipment. You will never hear back from them. If you wish, you can also contact the local British embassy or consulate and ask them if the supposed organisations are real. Don't forget that if something sounds too good to be true – that is probably because it really is too good to be true!

# 7. EXPORT PRICING

If you can count your money, then you are not really rich. (J. Paul Getty)

Finance is the art of passing currency from hand to hand until it finally disappears. (Robert W. Sarnoff)

It is always the best policy to tell the truth – unless of course you are an exceptionally good liar. (Jerome K. Jerome)

No matter what reason you have for wanting to export, at the end of the day you would like to make some money from the initiative. Maybe if you are merely looking to shift some surplus production, then your profit aspirations will be modest – but you still need to consider the following points before going ahead with price quotes.

Before drawing up price quotes or issuing a standard export price list, you must understand the following:-

**Positioning**

In chapter 3, I mentioned the importance of your positioning, and this has a significant effect on your pricing. In simple terms, you are High End, Mid-Range or Down Market. There is nothing right or wrong about operating in any of these sectors – as long as the positioning of your Four Ps (product, price, place and promotion) is consistent.

My advice is that you should start off with the intention of positioning yourself similar to where you are in your domestic market. Once all the numbers have been crunched, you may well have to compromise, but at least start off similar to your home market position. So, the final price to the end consumer should be somewhere akin to those competitors whose positioning is similar to yours.

My problem was always caused by the fact that in the U.K. my company's products were positioned alongside our German competitors, because our established brand was so strong. Outside the U.K. when we entered new markets, our unknown brand was perceived as being inferior to the Germans. So straight away we had to compromise.

Just remember that it is easy to re-position downwards but it is very difficult to re-position upwards – and can take years. Ask the people who re-positioned the Skoda brand.

Once you have compared your home market positioning and consumer prices with your competitors' activity in your target market, you can establish your own target end user prices in that market.

**Direct Costs**

In order to arrive at prices for an export market you must accept that in nearly every case the cost of producing your product or service will exceed the cost of producing your domestic market offering. The following list is typical of export product cost-adders:-

- Different grades of metal, plastic, paper
- Alternative parts, due to the need to remove any English-language text
- More expensive internal components (don't forget that alternative export components can be more expensive until increased volumes are achieved)
- More complex programming
- Additional features or accessories
- Alternative colours
- Different brands in some cases
- More beefed-up packaging
- Additional labels, instruction leaflets
- Any number of local compliance and code board issues

If any additional processes are deemed necessary, then the labour cost will increase, as will any variable overhead costs.

**Indirect Costs**

As well as identifying the direct costs of your export products or services, there are a number of other cost elements which must be factored into your calculations – some of which will never enter into your home market calculations. These are really important, so I will cover them individually.

**Incoterms**

If you only take one thing from this book, please let it be the fact that if an exporter ignores the significance of Incoterms, then that exporter is in deep trouble.

Incoterms are standard internationally-recognised Terms Of Trade which define the duties and responsibilities of both parties in an international transaction. They apply to goods only – not to services.

There are eleven Incoterms, all recognised by three letter abbreviations. The most basic is EXW (ex Works) which means that the importer pays for everything, all the exporter has to do is make the products available for collection by the importer's nominated carrier. The most complex is DDP (Delivered, Duty Paid), which means that the exporter pays for everything, even the import charges in the importer's country. The other nine Incoterms confirm who is responsible for each of the costs in the process. They are updated every ten years, the last time being in 2020.

Not every trader understands what each Incoterm means so, after issuing your export prices, you should check that your prospective customer realises which party is responsible for each element of cost in the process.

It is not right or wrong to insist upon any of these Incoterms. But it is vitally important that the relevant Term is clearly communicated and understood by the exporter, the importer and the carrier. The Incoterm should appear on all price quotes, order acknowledgements, shipping documents and invoices. Incoterms determine which party has to pay import duties so they must be correct if the goods are to clear customs in the importer's country.

## EXPLANATION OF INCOTERMS 2020 - WHO PAYS ?

| | EXW | FCA | FAS | FOB | CFR | CIF | CPT | CIP | DAP | DPU | DDP |
|---|---|---|---|---|---|---|---|---|---|---|---|
| Warehouse Storage & Labour | Seller | Seller | Seller | Seller | Seller | Seller | Seller | Seller | Seller | Seller | Seller |
| Export Packing | Seller | Seller | Seller | Seller | Seller | Seller | Seller | Seller | Seller | Seller | Seller |
| Loading & Customs Clearance | Buyer | Seller | Seller | Seller | Seller | Seller | Seller | Seller | Seller | Seller | Seller |
| Inland Haulage to Port | Buyer | Buyer | Seller | Seller | Seller | Seller | Seller | Seller | Seller | Seller | Seller |
| Terminal Charges | Buyer | Buyer | Seller | Seller | Seller | Seller | Seller | Seller | Seller | Seller | Seller |
| Forwarder's Charges | Buyer | Buyer | Seller | Seller | Seller | Seller | Seller | Seller | Seller | Seller | Seller |
| Loading On Vessel | Buyer | Buyer | Buyer | Seller | Seller | Seller | Seller | Seller | Seller | Seller | Seller |
| Ocean/Air Freight | Buyer | Buyer | Buyer | Buyer | Seller | Seller | Seller | Seller | Seller | Seller | Seller |
| Insurance | Buyer | Buyer | Buyer | Buyer | Buyer | Seller | Buyer | Seller | Seller | Seller | Seller |
| Charges Upon Arrival | Buyer | Buyer | Buyer | Buyer | Buyer | Buyer | Buyer | Buyer | Seller | Seller | Seller |
| Unloading Charges | Buyer | Buyer | Buyer | Buyer | Buyer | Buyer | Buyer | Buyer | Buyer | Seller | Buyer |
| Duty, Taxes & Customs Clearance | Buyer | Buyer | Buyer | Buyer | Buyer | Buyer | Buyer | Buyer | Buyer | Buyer | Seller |
| Inland Haulage to Destination | Buyer | Buyer | Buyer | Buyer | Buyer | Buyer | Buyer | Buyer | Buyer | Buyer | Seller |

## Rules Of Origin and Import Duties

When an Exporter sells products (not services) to a customer outside of the U.K., the Exporter has to clearly state the Country Of Origin of the goods in question. It is vital that Origin is accurately declared, because it will affect the levying of import duties in the Importer's country.

Just because an item has been assembled in the U.K. does not make it of British origin. The component parts may well have been imported from the other side of the world before the assembly exercise.

Rules Of Origin are complicated and they often involve detailed calculations before an accurate Country Of Origin can be declared. It is important that Exporters take the time to fully understand the Rules Of Origin and their application before quoting export prices. Identification of your relevant Commodity Codes (an internationally recognised system) is essential as these will determine which Rules Of Origin calculations apply to your products.

## Warranty Costs

You probably supply your products or services in your domestic market with a warranty but delivering a similar offer to export markets could be (a) expensive, (b) difficult or (c) impossible – so you will need to think things through.

Depending on your product or service, you need to establish how you will deal with warranty claims. Either you will have to send someone over to the export market, you will have to find and appoint someone locally to do it on your behalf, or you will supply your customer on ex warranty terms and let them deal with it. None of these is wrong just as long as you have agreed things up front before agreeing prices. If your customer is not going to pick up the responsibility, you will need to add a warranty provision in your costings.

## Currency Costs

One of the most crucial items to consider when selling abroad is which currency to use. The simplest way forward is to quote all prices in Sterling, and that will help your accountant to sleep at night!

But, as your relationship develops with your customer and you trade regularly in Sterling with that customer, I can guarantee that the first item on the agenda when you go to visit the customer will be the exchange rate. This means that every visit will start on poor terms, because the customer is immediately out to get a price reduction.

Export is no different to any other commercial activity – if you can make it easy for your customer to buy from you, then the relationship will benefit. The customer wants to know exactly how much they have to pay for their purchases, without regular fluctuation.

Where possible, I tried to quote my customers in their own currency, if their currency was one of the reliable ones – Euros, US Dollars, Canadian Dollars, Australian Dollars, Japanese Yen, Swiss Francs, Norwegian Kroner etc

If the customer's currency was less reliable then I would quote in Sterling. And, if the customer was unhappy with that, I would compromise with US Dollars or Euros.

When you are quoting in a non-Sterling currency, you will need to make a provision in your costings for fluctuations in the rate of exchange. You should also inform your bank before you start on foreign currency transactions.

## Payment Costs

International transactions use a number of different Terms Of Payment, some involving no period of credit and some involving credit of up to 180 days. The various Terms offer differing levels of risk for the seller. The safest of course is "Cash In Advance" and the riskiest is "Open Account". If a customer refuses to pay in advance, the next best option for the seller is "Confirmed Irrevocable Letter of Credit", which can give the customer a period of credit, whilst minimising the seller's risk.

I strongly recommend that you get credit insurance on transactions using less secure terms of payment. Of course, all insurance involves the paying of a premium – which needs to be included in your costings.

Some methods of payment will result in bank charges being made. I always worked with customers on the basis that any charges levied in the U.K. would be borne by us and any charges levied in the customer's country would be paid by them. This is fair and was accepted pretty much by everyone. Some U.K. accountants will refuse all charges, in which case you have to negotiate with your customer.

Some countries, particularly Germany, operate an early payment system called "Skonto". The buyer pays for the goods very early, typically after 7 or 14 days, and deducts a figure (usually 2 or 3%) from the total payable. Whenever I sold to mainland Europe, I kept 3% up my sleeve and if the customer raised the matter of "Skonto", I could agree to it. If they didn't ask, then I had the 3% up my sleeve for another day. This "Skonto" amount should be included in your costings.

As long as you have built it into your costings, there is no reason why you should not agree to "Skonto" – it guarantees early payment, after all.

## Local Taxes

Before you start to look at target end consumer prices, you need to understand what taxes are used in your target market. Earlier, I mentioned that Rules Of Origin issues may result in import duties being payable. You should find out in advance if that is the case, because it will help you to better understand the full landed cost of your items in your target market.

Once your customer has received your goods, local sales taxes must be applied before the end user takes ownership. In the case of countries like the U.S.A., there can be Federal (national) sales taxes as well as State sales taxes, but in most countries there is usually a single tax, such as VAT. You need to know what that figure is, in order to calculate the effect on your items.

## System Margins

We looked earlier at the various Routes To Market and we recognised that there are several links in the supply chain between you and your end user. Every one of those links needs an acceptable margin if the transaction is to be taken on board with enthusiasm. If an agent, a distributor or a retailer does not make enough from your offering, they simply will not give it their full support. So, you need to establish early on what margin is required by each link in the chain – and hopefully the system will still leave enough for you.

Margins fluctuate by country – and they do not all use the same calculation or terminology.

**What Do They Mean By "Margin"?**

Price from A to B          £100 plus 20% VAT

Price from B to C          £125 plus 20% VAT

B's **"Margin"** is          $(125 - 100 =) 25 \div 125 = \textbf{20\%}$
(this is also known as "Profit On Return")

B's **"Mark Up"** is          $(125 - 100 =) 25 \div 100 = \textbf{25\%}$

B's **"Coefficient"** is          $(125 \text{ plus } 20\% =) 150 \div 100 = \textbf{1.50}$

The Coefficient is used by many retailers, especially in France, Germany and the Benelux countries. It enables them to recognise very simply what retail price they can hit, based upon their buying price.

If a retailer usually operated on a coefficient of 1.65, it could quickly be seen that a buying price of €177.00 would generate a retail price of €292.05, which would then round up to €299.99.

Retailers won't only operate on one coefficient. They will look to maximise their profits at the higher end and accept lower coefficients at the more competitive budget end of the market.

None of these methods is right or wrong, but you need to understand which method your prospective partners know and apply.

**Price Lists**

At some stage in the proceedings, you will be expected to issue a Price List. This may be a "Standard Export Price List", which would be in sterling and using Ex Works terms. This would of course be loaded so that you can be negotiated downwards, after meaningful discussions on sales volumes and future relationships have taken place.

I used to issue two "Standard Export Price Lists" – one for Europe and North America, one for the Middle East and Africa. The reasoning was that while Europeans will expect you to drop by 5 to 15% in negotiations, the Middle Eastern buyers will expect 20 to 35% reductions. For buyers not wishing to commit to large quantities, or for buyers to whom you do not wish to confer an official representative status, then your Standard Export Price List would apply.

After fruitful discussions have taken place, you may choose to prepare a Price List for a specific buyer. This list would include whatever currency has been agreed and the appropriate Incoterm.

All Price Lists should be issued on your official headed stationery (hard copy or electronic) with your full contact details, registered company reference (if appropriate) and VAT registration number (with EORI number), if applicable.

If your products or services break down into logical categories or sub-groups, then lay out your lists in that way to make them easy to follow. I suggest that all your price lists should include the following:-

*Model or Product Reference* – these should be the same references used in your catalogues and on your website.

*Description* – without going into great detail, include a brief description, perhaps with basic dimensions (45cm, 13kg, 220 volts) or colours.

*Illustration* – in some cases you will choose to incorporate thumbnail photographs or line drawings to aid identification.

*Commodity Code* – this is the internationally-accepted code for each of your items and it enables both parties to understand what import duties may be levied.

*Country Of Origin* – do not guess at the country code. Satisfy yourself that you have completed any relevant origin calculations before declaring so on your price list.

*Incoterm, with named place* – this is an area where your buyer will almost certainly want to negotiate with you. Before declaring a term on your price list, make sure you understand to what you are committing. You cannot just state "EXW" or "DDP", you must state the name of the place where responsibility is handed over. So, it might be "Ex Works Manchester" or "DDP Milan" for instance. Incoterms are such an important element of international trade, so take time to understand them.

*Currency* – initially you should use Sterling prices, but this may change as you negotiate. Incidentally, I once saw some research which showed that people are more inclined to negotiate rounded prices than unrounded. So, £300 will be challenged, whereas £295.38 or £308.54 may not be!

*Terms Of Payment* – my advice when just starting out with a prospective buyer is to ask for cash in advance until a trading history is established. This will not appeal to many buyers, so see on which terms you can get credit insurance. If the buyer's business is very new, or if there is a poor credit rating, you may have to stay with cash in advance or

Confirmed Irrevocable Letter of Credit (CILC). In many cases, you can get credit insurance on reasonable terms like 60 days open account. Do not allow yourself to be bullied into an open account arrangement if it is not covered by credit insurance.

If you need to insist upon a CILC, this is the most secure method of payment, other than cash up front. It is very safe – but you have to deliver everything exactly as stipulated in the wording of the CILC. Before signing a CILC, in the early days ask your bank and your carrier to scrutinise the wording, to make sure that you can actually do everything mentioned – particularly when it comes to the presentation of certain documents by certain times.

*Time Period* – you need to state how long your quoted prices will remain valid. Once you have started working with an overseas partner, you are not going to win many favours by increasing prices midway through a selling season. Try to give your buyers as much stability as possible, whilst not leaving yourself too vulnerable to exchange rate fluctuations. I found that 6 months often worked. However, some customers insisted on a full 12 months fixed price, especially if the products were included in seasonal catalogues. Sometimes your representatives will have to honour pricing commitments and you will have to support them.

*Your Customers' Prices* – the price lists which you issue include your prices to your customers. You cannot dictate to your customers what their selling prices must be, neither can you dictate what the end price to the consumer must be. Retail Price Maintenance is prohibited in most sophisticated markets. You can discuss consumer prices with your customers, especially as you strive to understand the margins in the system – but you should avoid any correspondence which suggests that you are trying to influence the prices at which your customers sell.

# 8. PREPARING FOR THAT FIRST OVERSEAS TRIP

If it takes you more than fifteen minutes to pack, then you have too much stuff. (Mother Teresa)

It used to be a good hotel, but that proves nothing – I used to be a good boy. (Mark Twain)

Flying? I have been to almost as many places as my luggage. (Bob Hope)

You cannot export from behind a desk. At some stage you are going to get on a plane, board a ferry or use the Channel Tunnel to visit your prospective trading partners and see for yourself the market in which they operate. The first visit is vitally important as you seek to create positive first impressions.

Before you leave the U.K., your prospective partners will probably have certain expectations of a "typical" British business person. They think you will be:-

- Punctual
- Courteous
- Honest
- Well-prepared
- Possibly risk-averse
- Perhaps predictable
- Poor linguistically

So, if that is what they are expecting, you have to confirm the good things and disprove the bad ones.

**Punctuality**

We are known the world over for being on time. Our foreign business contacts are expecting us to be punctual – so you can already bank that one. Do not drop your standards but go out of your way to maintain that most desirable of reputations.

To get to your first meeting, you will have had to plan plane times, hotel reservations, taxi rides, and maybe train journeys. Be pedantic when checking the details – how far is it between stages, how long will it take and what alternatives do you have? Invariably there will be long periods of inactivity between the various stages but try to avoid giving yourself a schedule which is too tight. If your first plane is late arriving, will you miss your connecting flight? How long might it take to travel by taxi (or hire car) across a large city in the rush hour? Be strict with yourself and do not risk being late.

You should avoid flying to your destination on the morning of your meeting, as you could well arrive late. And you should avoid meetings on the same day you arrive on a long flight. Travel the evening before, get a decent night's sleep in a local hotel then go to your meeting refreshed and ready for action.

I can only really remember being late for an overseas appointment twice. Evans and I had to get from Prague to Brno for the start of an exhibition. Our distributor sent one of his drivers in a dodgy Skoda and we then travelled through an unexpectedly nasty April blizzard on unprepared roads. A journey of two hours took over four hours, but we were lucky. A car not long behind us left the road and its occupants were killed.

Evans was involved in the second incident, and that time it was his fault! We were going to an important meeting with Thomson Brandt, the leading French appliances manufacturer, in Paris. We left the station, jumped in a taxi and Evans explained in French that we wished to go to Avenue General Leclerc. Our expected fifteen minute journey had taken nearly thirty minutes when we discovered that we were being taken to a different Avenue General Leclerc, on the opposite side of the city.

From that day onwards, irrespective of the linguistic abilities of my colleagues, I always wrote down the full address (complete with postal code) for taxi drivers.

Often, your business contacts will offer to collect you from your hotel, or railway station, or airport. I never liked my customers to collect me on the evening prior to our meeting, because you end up discussing some of the points you will be covering in a more structured way the following day.

On one occasion, my Maltese customer sent his daughter to collect me from the airport. So, I was whisked across the island by probably the best-looking young woman in Malta, in her open-topped sports car. I got a few looks!

When I first visited Greece, my host told me that we would eat later in the evening. His colleague whispered that when he says "evening" he probably means "tomorrow". Sure enough, we ate half an hour after midnight and finished off in an ice cream parlour at 3am. With one or two exceptions, the Greeks were the most unpunctual people I worked with, but the blighters used to get away with it by saying "Mike, you worry too much, it will be ok in the end". I don't think that "chaos" is a Greek word, but it certainly ought to be! In fact it would make a perfect name for a little Greek island.

For my first visit to Hong Kong, I was to be collected from the foyer of my hotel by a new colleague whom I had not met previously. I asked how I would recognise her. "Oh, easy – I am 5 feet 2 inches and Chinese", she said. Unfortunately, so was everyone else in the foyer that day!

I managed to discover a number of ways to save time and money, not least of which was in travelling to Jerusalem from the airport at Tel Aviv. A passenger next to me told me to avoid the expensive buses just outside the airport doors, but instead to turn right and locate a couple of minibuses which used to drop off at the various hotels at a fraction of the price. I used these minibuses every time thereafter, although as the only Gentile on board it seemed as though I was always the last one to be dropped off!

Sometimes my punctuality had unforeseen benefits. I had arranged a meeting in Vienna in the afternoon of 20th April 1989 (the date is significant) and the plan was to fly in the evening to Salzburg, in time for a meeting the next morning. My perfect plans were thrown into disarray when the afternoon meeting was called off, so I cancelled my flight and took a train to Salzburg. The train journey from Vienna to Salzburg was the most picturesque I have ever encountered, absolutely beautiful scenery. The only macabre aspect of the journey was that I had been within one hour of Braunau (Hitler's birthplace) on the hundredth anniversary of his birth.

Occasionally my perfect planning has not been matched by my colleagues. I was involved in an attempted joint venture in Ukraine and to support my intended colleagues I had some good quality printed material sent out in good time for an exhibition in Kiev. I arrived by plane the night before the exhibition and then took a taxi to the exhibition grounds in good time on the opening morning of the event – only to discover that the show had been cancelled the night before! Apparently, there had been a shortage of aircraft fuel so all internal flights had been cancelled and the planned exhibitors could not get around. No-one had taken the trouble to tell me, although I was probably in the air when the announcement was made.

**Courtesy and Honesty**

Your hosts will expect you to demonstrate these two qualities, so don't let yourself down. Saying "please" and "thank you", holding doors open and similar gestures will be well-received. It costs nothing to be polite and you should build on this perceived piece of "Britishness".

Your host will expect you to be honest and that you will do exactly what you have promised to do. If you find that you are going to struggle to complete something in time for an agreed deadline, my advice is to tell the other party as soon as you can, to give them time to make any necessary adjustments to their plans.

On the theme of honesty, never forget that you are bound by the terms of the U.K. Bribery Act. You must not give nor receive bribes, neither must you stand by whilst your agents or representatives indulge in bribery. Rather than allow or condone acts of bribery, you should simply lose the order.

On the wall of his office, Evans had a framed cheque for £1000 – an attempted bribe from one of our customers, who became an ex-customer soon afterwards.

Take care not to receive too much hospitality from your hosts, who will hopefully become your business partners. When you are visiting someone else's country, it is fine for your host to pay for a meal, but you should not let them pay for your hotel. Make it clear from the outset that accepting the gift of a bottle of wine is fine, but a wristwatch clearly is not. You have to lay down the ground rules but without offending your hosts.

Similarly, if they come to the U.K., you can pay for meals and take them around in your car but be careful not to give any hint of a bribe. Souvenirs from the area in which you are located can be nice gestures, as long as they are not too expensive. One of our factories was situated near Stoke-on-Trent, so modest pieces of Wedgwood did the job.

## Preparation

We have a deserved reputation for being well-prepared and your first visit is a great opportunity to prove to your new partner how organised you are.

On another trip I made with Evans to Paris, we clearly misunderstood the nature of the meeting. We expected a brief "overview" meeting at which we would agree basic plans for development over the coming weeks. Our hosts had prepared detailed presentations, pulling in their relevant Product Managers as required. We just presented the same acetate to cover all four product groups. This was not our finest hour – although we did make amends at the second meeting!

It is always important to "check your props" beforehand. Any presentational aids or devices must be tested before you go live. Before travelling, check that your host has whatever you need – screens, projectors, adaptors, flipcharts, speakers, printers, internet access etc.

On a visit to Istanbul, I realised whilst still in the air that I had forgotten my phone charger. Upon arriving at my hotel, I explained my predicament to the hotel concierge – who just happened to be the world's most helpful man. He found out the nearest Nokia dealer, called them to check that they had a charger in stock and then wrote all the details down for a taxi driver. The taxi took me to the dealer, waited while I was served, and then brought me back to the hotel. I can't remember what tip I gave, but it was damned good value!

Evans and I started presenting a new washing machine to our distributor's staff in Warsaw when we discovered that we couldn't open the door! A part had broken while the product was in transit, so we needed screwdrivers and pliers to get ourselves out of trouble. Not the best first impression.

I have already mentioned the different ways of interpreting "margin" and it is important that you find out in advance of your first visit how your target market does this. Similarly, you should understand the negotiating expectations of your prospective partner – what will they be expecting you to concede from your standard prices?

## Risk-Taking and Predictability

Americans, in particular, regard the British as being risk-averse. After all, we were the ones who stayed behind when "The Mayflower" set sail on its adventure! If you are to lose this tag, you must be prepared to at least be seen to be considering movement from your starting position.

Similarly, you should conduct research so that you can go along to your first meeting with a surprise in store. This might be a special introductory offer, unexpected training support, extended warranties or local-language brochures. Quote examples of positive actions you have taken over the years when you stole a march on your competitors.

Examples of creative and forward-looking thinking will be well-received, so take suitable material with you.

## Poor Linguists

The British have developed a deserved reputation over the years for poor linguistic ability, so this is a big opportunity for you to surprise and impress your prospective partners. You are not going to become fluent in another language by merely attending a few evening classes and listening to some CDs. Once you have decided that your business is going to take on the challenge of export, you should positively discriminate in favour of candidates with language skills in the recruitment process. Encourage your younger members of staff to learn new languages.

Our problem is that the rest of the world regards English as its natural second language, especially when it comes to business. Many business people around the world speak very good English, so there is not a lot of incentive for us to learn other languages. I have often witnessed Koreans speaking English with Italians in hotel lobbies.

But which should be our natural second business language? I once read an article by a "futurist" who made a number of business predictions. He claimed that in 25 years' time the main business languages will be English, Spanish, Arabic and Mandarin. Meanwhile our future captains of industry are in school, learning French and German!

If nothing else, you should embrace "The Magnificent Seven", which I mentioned in chapter 6, plus some numbers in the local language. And a brief introductory presentation in the local lingo always goes down well. The more language work you do, the better you will be received – and of course it will help you when travelling, eating and buying. At least make an effort and avoid coming across as insular.

Already in this chapter I have stressed the need for research before making that all-important first visit but I have only scratched the surface regarding what you should research, therefore I will follow up now with the other areas you should research vigorously.

**Climate, Culture and Religion**

There are no "right people" and "wrong people" on this planet – just "different people". You will perform far more impressively if you find out how your customers are different and why they act as they do. Very often it is because of where they are located, what they do and what they believe.

You should find out the history of the country and its people, how its climate has influenced the lifestyle of the residents, how a previous colonial power has affected the country's development and how natural resources (oil, timber, rubber) may have caused booms and slumps over the generations.

 Understanding local culture will enable you to see how local customers think and why they may do things slightly differently. Of course, if you are appointing an agent or a distributor, they will already have that appreciation but the more you understand, the more of a contribution you will make.

The local religion will have a substantial effect on the lifestyle, practices, diet, seasonal events and attitudes of the people, who will be potential users of your products or services. You should research, understand and respect the local religion if you are to succeed.

The local climate often caught me out, particularly warmer climates. I was to deliver a presentation to a group of retailers in Thessaloniki, probably about 6.30pm in September and I turned up in a suit and tie. I had neatly typed out my script and had highlighted the important bits. But, when I stood up to deliver at the lectern, a sweat droplet fell from my brow, then another, and then one more. My script was severely smudged, so I had to deliver most of my presentation from memory. From that day, I always laminated my presentations in warmer countries.

During my first visit to Japan, I met my hosts from the Toshiba company in the city of Nagoya and they took me to see one of their factories nearby. Upon our return I used the second half of my rail ticket, which had been in my shirt pocket on this very humid day. I am afraid that my damp ticket briefly shut down the entire ticketing concourse in Nagoya station – which my hosts seemed to find amusing.

As an ice-breaker and as an illustration that you have done your homework, you could check the local news in the country to which you will be travelling and make a note of something topical. But be careful not to shoot yourself in the foot. Do not comment on anything political and avoid praising the wrong football team – telling your host in Barcelona how well Real Madrid played at the weekend will not do you any favours!

## Business Culture, Language and Etiquette

As well as personal differences in the way that people behave, you will come across many differences in the way that business is conducted.

In my experience, one of the biggest mistakes made by British exporters is by trying to enter the American market, thinking that the business culture there will be the same as in the U.K. In chapter 12, I explain why the business culture in America is very different – and therefore why British exporters need to change.

Small markets are like villages – everyone knows everyone else. So, if you travel to places like Cyprus, Malta or Iceland, your competitors' representatives will know you are there – and they will probably know where you are staying!

I found the South Koreans very good to deal with, being hardworking and reliable – but once the business has been done, they love to party! In Seoul, after a particularly fruitful meeting, I was taken for a Korean barbecue, which involved food cooked in front of you and the drinking of what they referred to as "local wine" but was in fact lethal firewater! Because of my inability to cope with the small, metal chopsticks, I was allowed to use the type of wooden training chopsticks that they give to their children. After the meal, we went to a karaoke bar – where it was compulsory to stand up and sing, whilst accompanied on the microphones by scantily-clad young ladies. Thankfully my version of "House Of The Rising Sun" was not recorded.

Had I researched local etiquette more thoroughly before my first visit to Dubai, I could have avoided an embarrassing incident. A group of us were taken up the Dubai Creek in a converted dhow and the order of the day was to sit on the floor of the vessel – but not showing the soles of shoes, which I had done. This is very offensive to Arabs, thankfully my embarrassing error was pointed out by a colleague quite early in proceedings.

The Basques are very proud of their heritage and enjoy a certain amount of autonomy. So they took great delight in pointing out to me that the Welsh flag has the same colours as their beloved Ikurrina flag.

Iceland is a country where the business people are straight-talking and reliable but they are also great hosts who love showing you their beautiful country. I was taken to see the original "geyser" and I also saw an absolutely enormous snowman in Akureyri, located in the north of the country, not too far from the Arctic Circle. The first time I met one of my Icelandic contacts was at the airport and told him not to call me "Mister Stokes" but to use "Mike". He replied by saying "my name is silly". I said, "that is ok, I don't mind, what is your name?" He explained that it was "Sigurdur Helgason", but everyone called him "Silli".

Silli was a jazz drummer and I was able to repay his hospitality when he came to London. I took him to Ronnie

Scott's Jazz Club and after the show I introduced him to the star of the evening, Georgie Fame.

When researching local etiquette, you should spend some time finding out about gestures and how they vary around the world. It is easy to offend someone quite unintentionally by the use of a gesture. I found a very useful book on this subject, "The Do's And Taboos Of Body Language Around The World" by Roger E. Axtell. Among the many instances are:-

- Do not touch an Arab with your left hand, as they think it is for "lavatorial" use
- Avoid using the thumbs up gesture, as it can often mean the same as an extended middle finger
- Stroking your chin can suggest in some cultures that you fancy someone
- Avoid the two-fingered "peace" sign as it means something very different the other way round
- In some parts of the Balkans and Middle East, nodding one's head can mean "No", whilst shaking one's head from side to side means "Yes"
- Check how firm handshakes are regarded. They are a sign of confidence in some countries, but are seen as an intimidating gesture in others
- Forming a circle with your thumb and forefinger means "ok" in North America and the UK but in some countries it can be interpreted as a private bodily orifice
- When you are travelling abroad, do your research and keep your fingers to yourself!

## Business Card Culture

There has been a trend, probably since the beginning of the Covid lockdown, to dispense with business cards – and it is seen as a modern thing to do. Take my advice, if you are dealing with overseas markets then you must use business cards, and you must learn how to use them.

Business cards are still a very important element of international trade communications and you will be expected to provide one whenever you meet with a prospective customer, supplier or intermediary. Because they are still important, you should ensure that your cards are of good quality, legible (avoid trendy silver print on black backgrounds) and of a standard size. I know that marketing advisers will tell you to produce business cards which are different – circular, triangular, bigger sizes etc. Believe me, if your customers cannot get your card in their business card folder or box, it will get thrown away.

Using my "Greenwich Meridian" theory, the further East you progress, the more your business cards are respected. When presenting your business card to someone based in the Far East, especially Japan, present it slowly with both hands, printed side uppermost and maybe with a slight bow. You should receive a business card with great respect, scrutinising the print and regarding it as a fine piece of art or jewellery.

Do NOT disrespect a business card, do NOT write on the face of a business card and do NOT flippantly stuff it in your back pocket. These actions will offend the person from whom you have received the card, and straight away you have managed to get off to a bad start.

## Local Markets, Local Players and Partner Data

Before visiting a new market for the first time, it is vital that you conduct lots of research and don't just rely upon your prospective partner to tell you everything. Of course your prospective partners will want to impress you with their knowledge and supposed market influence but you need to double check what they are saying. Some of the data they provide could well be delivered with a hidden agenda, which will aid them when you come to sit down and negotiate.

Try to find out the approximate size of the market you are visiting, and don't just assume that the market size will be in proportion to the population – climate, politics and prosperity can influence things. As well as the market size, try to recognise any trends – growth, contraction, shifts by sector or segment. If you can pick up any data on local pricing, then even better.

If I had done better research before my first trip to Jakarta, I would have known that my British passport needed to have over 6 months to run, in order to avoid the need for a visa. Mine didn't, so let us just say that I had to enter into a bout of creative negotiating with the immigration official.

The local market players may not be the ones against whom you compete in the U.K., indeed you may not have heard of them before. Any data you can glean will stand you in good stead as you approach the first meeting.

Try to find out where your prospective partners are active, if they attend exhibitions or conferences, if their website is consistent with your positioning and, of course, how financially stable they are.

You must be fully-prepared before you make that first visit. Don't wing it!

## Things To Check Before Leaving

To ensure that you arrive fully-briefed and equipped, I suggest the following checklist, which is not comprehensive because there will be variations by region:-

*Samples* – if you are taking samples, you need the right paperwork to clear customs. If you are sending samples, make sure that they arrive before you do.

*Props* – check you have everything you will need during the meeting (colour swatches, examples of components, electric plug convertors, items in the local language) because you cannot just pop back to the office afterwards.

*Visual Aids* – if you are delivering presentations, or maybe showing TV or Radio Adverts, check in advance the availability of the relevant kit.

*Documentation* – take whatever documents you may wish to refer to during your meeting, for example prices quoted, costings, correspondence, sales brochures and prospectuses, technical manuals, compliance certificates.

*Phone* – make sure you can stay in contact, so check the availability of phone signals, availability of WiFi calling, roaming charges etc. Do not forget your phone charger.

*Broadband, WiFi and Bluetooth* – you will want to be available whilst you are abroad, so check local connectivity. If you are taking laptops or tablets with you, then do not forget the chargers.

*Draft Agreement* – depending upon the amount of contact you have already had with your prospective partner, you might be in a position to discuss the formalising of your relationship. It would be prudent therefore to take a draft agreement with you.

To avoid setting up an official agreement too early in proceedings, I often used a Memorandum Of Understanding. This is a brief summary, usually for a period of about 6 months before a more formal agreement is set up. Likely areas for inclusion would be:-

- Names and Addresses of the two parties
- Territory
- Brands and Products
- Pricing
- Orders, Deliveries, Stockholding
- Returns
- Marketing, Promotions and Showrooms
- Payments
- Warranty and After Sales Service
- Ethics (especially the U.K. Bribery Act)
- Intellectual Property
- Confidentiality
- Duration
- Termination

Any document (MOU or Agreement) must clearly state that it is governed by the laws of England and Wales – or the laws of Scotland if that is where you are based.

Beware of any Memorandum Of Understanding which is stuck in front of you and which confers exclusivity. If you wish to demonstrate your commitment to an agent, distributor or reseller, then make sure that you use the term **"sole" and not "exclusive".** "Sole" means that you will not give a similar commitment to anyone else in the market. "Exclusive" means that you will not supply your products to anyone else in that market – even if your official partner has stopped paying you! I once had a German distributor who decided to stop paying, so we found a way of supplying their biggest retail customer directly. It was extra work for us, but it maintained a continuity of supply to the market.

*Contact with British Embassy* – it makes sense to contact the local British diplomatic post before travelling. This may be an Embassy, a Consulate or a High Commission. They will be genuinely interested in what you are doing and why you are going there. They can also give you some valuable information on the political situation, the current financial situation and tips on how to do business in that part of the world. They may give you an hour in their offices when you arrive, designed to help you to walk into the market with your eyes open. And they may even know your prospective trading partner.

Embassy contact is essential if you are intending to visit potentially dangerous areas, so be open about your travel plans and timings.

I developed a particularly close relationship with the British Embassy in Athens over the years, to the extent that they often used to forward translated newspaper and trade magazine articles. By the same token, they often asked me to speak with British businesses who were looking to start in the Greek market.

## My "Greenwich Meridian" Theory

When you are researching other markets, and while you are evaluating prospective trading partners, don't forget that they are scrutinising you as well. They want to be sure that you will be a reliable and reputable principal, so they will take their time to get to know you.

If you take the Meridian which runs through Greenwich and look towards the East, you will discover two significant facts:-

1. The further you go, the longer it takes for business people to trust you
2. The further you go, the more important it is for business people to trust you

By the time you reach Japan, it is imperative that you build that trust – but it will take a long time, and several visits, before you earn that trust. It is normal for Finance Directors (who pay the travel bills) to lose patience long before your prospective Japanese customer has signed up.

**Being British**

All the time that you are travelling and meeting people, you are representing your business and hopefully creating a good impression so that business will get done. But you are also representing something far bigger than your own business – you are representing your country!

By being professional and polished you will create a good impression of the U.K. and this will not only help your own business aspirations, it will help all the Brits who come after you.

# 9. NEGOTIATING WITH DIFFERENT CULTURES

Be understanding of one another – be willing to compromise. (Yoko Ono)

When a man tells me he is going to put all his cards on the table, I always look up his sleeve. (Lord Hore-Belisha)

Fear the Greeks bearing gifts. (Proverb)

No matter whether you are negotiating in the U.K., in English, or negotiating in a foreign country via an interpreter – you will go through the same seven stages of negotiation. These are:-

1. *Prepare* (know what you want, understand each other's position and identify any differences)
2. *Open* (put cases forward and understand issues)
3. *Clarify* (support cases, challenge and discuss)
4. *Explore* (probe possibilities, observe behaviour)
5. *Bargain* (assemble potential trades, make bids)
6. *Close* (build commitment, reach agreement)
7. *Sustain* (ensure it all happens)

Although the stages are the same, there are many differences in the way that business people abroad approach negotiations and in the way that business people abroad perform during negotiations. There is no "right" and "wrong" but there are differences and you need to understand these differences before you sit down to negotiate.

The party with the most **information** is normally the one which takes most away from a negotiation, so it is vital that you prepare fully beforehand. As well as knowing about your prospective partner and the market in which they operate, make sure that you are fully familiar with your product offering, the costs thereof and your minimum "walk away point".

You need to gauge the other party's mindset and their **expectations**. What would be a good result for them? How badly do they need to do a deal with you? What happens if there is no deal?

**Punctuality** is important. You can really start off on the wrong foot if you turn up late. Being early creates a very positive impression – the other party feels that they are dealing with someone who is well-organised and reliable. I was once asked to go to London to meet with some Iraqi buyers and the meeting point was at 8am in the foyer of a hotel. I was determined not to be late, so took the early train and I was sitting in the hotel foyer by 7.30am. No-one had shown up so at 9am I got a phone call informing me that the meeting had been moved to a different hotel. I took three more such calls, each one changing the time and venue. I was eventually seen at 4.30pm, tired, frustrated and annoyed. To cap it all, they showed little or no interest in my products!

The trickiest challenge I faced during my time in exporting was to go to Argentina and re-energise a distributor who had experienced some product reliability issues and who was threatening us with a $250,000 legal claim. I recognised the need to get all of their issues out on the table so, despite the tiring 13 hour flight we had experienced, my colleague and I agreed to an early meeting, rather than let tensions continue. The businesslike "can do" approach we demonstrated really impressed the local distributor and we were able to maintain this goodwill throughout our stay. The bottom line was that the settlement only cost us £20,000 – and that was product value, not cash. Where possible, I settled all disputes by means of supplying products rather than cash. The perceived value (which is your selling price) is always higher than the cost to you, so you should avoid agreeing cash settlements. Before visiting any new country for the first time I always sat down with my shipping colleagues. I needed to understand how our products would get from our premises to the customer's premises, and at what cost. I wanted to be aware of any anomalies that might be thrown at me, so that I could respond with confidence and I was keen to know if local customs were likely to be over zealous in their dealings with our shippers.

Because you have done your research, you will know how **greetings** should be handled. As we have seen, in Far Eastern countries it is the ritual to observe and respect each other's business cards.

Find out whether gifts are expected at a first meeting, and whether it is customary to exchange pleasantries before doing business. In some countries, it is normal to ask after each other's families, so do your homework beforehand.

It is normal that water and soft **drinks** are provided, but I always used to take a small bottle of water in my bag, just in case. I advise you strongly not to take alcoholic drinks before or during a meeting, even if the other party indulges.

I was taken to meet a retailer in Santarem, Portugal, where it is customary to take food before a meeting. The food consisted of a local soup, which included a complete pig's ear for flavour. I have a strong constitution but that was a real test!

The points above are all designed to ensure you sit down at the negotiating table fully-prepared and having created a positive impression with your customer. But what about your performance during the actual negotiation?

After introductions have been made, try to establish pretty soon the **seniority** of the various participants. In some cultures, it is fine for you to address the most relevant person at the table but, in other cultures, you will be expected only to address the most senior person present.

I attended a meeting in Tokyo with nineteen executives from the Toshiba group – just me and nineteen of them! I managed to arrange their business cards on the table in front of me, so I wouldn't forget the relative seniority.

Once you have established how senior people are, it is important to maintain eye contact with the most senior person, even if you are speaking through an interpreter. Whether you are speaking through an interpreter or not, it is important to speak slowly – even if you are nervous. And avoid too many idioms, sayings and colloquialisms if you want to be understood.

Having said that you need to understand who is in the room with you, some businesses will operate a **"shuttle"** tactic with you. This can test your stamina, as they will take it in turns to disappear (and take refreshments) and be replaced by someone fresh. I found that some German companies, in particular, used this tactic. Don't be afraid to request a break so that you are just as refreshed as they are.

You should be bursting with **positivity** and creativity as you enter into negotiations. Try to avoid saying "no" to requests for concessions, instead saying that it can be looked at – and, of course, you can then seek reciprocal concessions. You will be respected by being creative and finding ways around roadblocks in the conversation.

Demonstrate flexibility during the conversation. You should find the middle road between being persistent and being annoying. Persistent negotiators believe that eventually you will give in just so they will shut up. The most persistent negotiators I met were Israelis. They developed persistence into an art form, even begging me for another two per cent as they waved me off at the airport departure gate!

Equally persistent, but seriously under-estimated, are the Irish. They would argue, but not in an aggressive way. Then they would deliberately misunderstand something and by the time all had been clarified, you had agreed to something else! Managing to confuse Ex Works prices with delivered prices was a favourite.

Try to stay calm during negotiations, avoiding aggression and **forcefulness**. Stand your ground and be assertive but the idea is not to intimidate the other party. Do not display anger, even if the other party is being unreasonable.

Your research will have taught you about the culture of your new market, and their attitude towards **concessions**. If you sit down with a Dutch buyer, he will feel insulted if you talk to him about thirty per cent price reductions. However, if you meet with a buyer from the Middle East, that buyer will expect to see concessions of thirty per cent, and will feel insulted by a "derisory" offer of ten per cent. It is important that you know beforehand which type of buyer you are meeting.

Irrespective of which sort of buyer you are meeting, you must understand where your **walk away point** is. If you go below your walk away point, two things will happen:-

1. You will make little or no money from the deal
2. The situation will rankle with you and you will be very reluctant to give much support to the activity

Most unsatisfactory negotiations are the result of misunderstandings by one party or both. Someone will think they have agreed to something – but, in reality, they haven't. The best way to avoid this is to regularly **summarise** during the meeting what both parties have agreed so far. And, at the end of the meeting, all agreed points should be listed, clarified and confirmed.

Negotiations should not be rushed, misunderstandings can occur if things are rushed. Give yourselves plenty of **time** to fully discuss each point.

As soon after the meeting as possible, all agreed action points should be **communicated** to the other party. And then the funs starts, as both parties seek to sustain what has been agreed.

The following chart lists the type of business behaviour applicable to the various parts of the world. Of course, it is a generalisation, but it is a useful guide. It is based on a book called "Cross Cultural Business Behaviour" by Richard R. Gesteland.

# CROSS-CULTURAL BUSINESS BEHAVIOUR

| | Deal-focussed (straight into business, no small talk, time matters) / Relationship-focused (personal and family issues discussed, time taken to earn mutual trust) | Formal (Handshakes, suits, cards, "Mr", status matters) / Informal (first name terms, smart casual, egalitarian) | Monochronic (Rigid Time) (punctual, time respected, agenda, no interruptions) / Polychronic (Fluid Time) (often late, less rigid agenda, frequent interruptions) | Expressive (animated, passionate, lots of touching, volatile) / Reserved (polite, unruffled, not much touching, no display of emotions) |
|---|---|---|---|---|
| **Group A** Bangladesh, Burma, Cambodia, India, Indoneseia, Laos, Malaysia, Pakistan, Philippines, Sri Lanka, Thailand, Vietnam and most sub-Saharan African countries | Relationship-focused | Formal | Polychronic | Reserved |
| **Group B** China, Japan, Singapore, South Korea | Relationship-focused | Formal | Monochronic | Reserved |
| **Group C** Arab Countries, Brazil, Croatia, Egypt, Greece, Latin America, Mexico, Serbia, Slovenia, Turkey | Relationship-focused | Formal | Polychronic | Expressive |
| **Group D** Bulgaria, Poland, Romania, Russia, Slovakia | Relationship-focused | Formal | Polychronic | Variably Expressive |
| **Group E** Belgium, France, Hungary, Italy, Portugal, Spain | Moderately Deal-focussed | Formal | Variably Monochronic | Emotionally Expressive |
| **Group F** Baltic States | Moderately Deal-focussed | Formal | Variably Monochronic | Reserved |
| **Group G** Austria, Czech Republic, Denmark, Finland, Germany, Great Britain, Ireland, Netherlands, Norway, Sweden, Switzerland | Deal-focused | Moderately Formal | Monochronic | Reserved |
| **Group H** Australia, Canada, New Zealand, USA and parts of South Africa | Deal-focused | Informal | Monochronic | Variably Expressive |
| **Group I** Israel | Deal-focused | Formal | Variably Monochronic | Emotionally Expressive |

*The Source of the above chart is "Cross-Cultural Business Behavior" by Richard R. Gesteland (Copenhagen Business School Press, 2012)*

## The Exporter's Negotiation Package

When any business people walk into a negotiation room, they have a number of elements with which to bargain or trade. Depending upon the seniority of the individuals, these may include product prices, quantity discount, turnover rebate and period of credit. But because of the relative complexity of export transactions, you will have far more bargaining tools upon which to call when you are negotiating with an export customer,

*Products* – unlike domestic negotiations where product specifications are pretty much fixed, when dealing with export customers you have more scope to explore various modifications. It is important therefore to take critical cost data with you, so you can understand the implications of each conceded modification.

*Prices* – having pointed out the need to understand your foreign customer's expectations on concessions, you need to establish in your own mind before you start (a) what is an ideal price, (b) what is an acceptable price and (c) what is the absolute walk away price.

*Currencies* – conceding that you will charge in the local currency may not actually cost you much, but it can be perceived as quite a valuable tool if you are getting bogged down in a negotiation.

*Discounts and Rebates* – it is unlikely that you will discuss incentives at early meetings, but they could come into play at a later date. Rather than just be based upon sales volumes, you can use such methods to reward listings through certain channels, distribution by region and even to reward activity on your more highly-specified items.

*Incoterms* – if you clearly understand what each Incoterm covers, you can vary the Incoterm as a method of trading during a negotiation. In order to accept a price concession, you may counteract by stating that the terms be changed from FOB to EXW or maybe from DDP to DAP. Conversely, if you are asked to accept a different Incoterm, you must confirm who therefore is going to pay for what. Some customers may refer to traditional old terms like "Cash Against Documents". You need to understand what they mean, then convert what they are saying into current Incoterms language. But, once you have done that, just check that both parties still agree exactly who is paying for what.

*Terms of Payment* – the scope you have to vary the Terms of Payment will depend upon the credit insurance you have set up. Try to get credit insurance on longer terms than you need initially, and then you have some room for manoeuvre. So, if you get insurance cover on "90 days Open Account", you can start off by offering "60 days Open Account" and allow yourself to be moved up to 90 days during the negotiation if needs be.

*Warranty* – whether you are selling goods or services, somewhere there will be an end user who receives a guarantee – and someone has to cover the cost of honouring that guarantee. Depending upon the sector in which you operate, there may be well-established rules on this responsibility – but, if not, this may be an area that is negotiable. You need to fully understand the local practice and the cost of matching it.

*Training Support* – it is normal that your overseas trading partner will have a need for staff training, both sales training and technical training. But, whether the trainer goes abroad or the overseas staff come to the U.K., there will be costs involved – flights, taxis, hotels, meals etc. You should evaluate those costs before over-promising at the negotiation table.

*Promotional and Launch Support* – depending upon your reason for exporting, you may wish to support your partners launch activity and you may be expected to contribute an initial promotional gesture. Consider such expenditure beforehand, so that you are not surprised when you sit down to negotiate.

So, there are plenty of things for the exporter to use when negotiating. It is a question of walking into things with both eyes open and understanding all relevant costs before you start bargaining.

# 10. EFFECTIVE USE OF OVERSEAS TRADE SHOWS

Nothing is more humiliating than to see idiots succeed with enterprises in which we have failed. (Gustave Flaubert)

I have written complete books on advertising – cheque books (Lord Sugar)

The only reason I made a commercial for American Express was to pay for my American Express bill. (Peter Ustinov)

I have long been an advocate of overseas exhibitions, as long as they are used effectively. I don't mean casually turning up with no real objectives, I mean the structured and monitored use of exhibitions.

Exhibitions, including conferences and similar events, can be used in a variety of ways, and I would like to look at how they can be used in these four ways:-
1. Using Exhibition Data For Research
2. Visiting Exhibitions To Find Representatives
3. Visiting Exhibitions To Support Representatives
4. Exhibiting Yourselves (Regionally or Globally)

**Using Exhibition Data For Research**

This is where I fall out with Market Research purists. They claim that exhibitions are not valid sources of research data because they are all about aspirations and not facts. I argue that exhibitions give you an idea of trends and therefore likely future products. So you can establish with what you will have to compete going forwards, and not just with what you could have competed in the past.

I have regularly stressed the need for research at every stage before visiting overseas markets. You will have used online directories, perhaps purchased tailored market data, used third party consultants and maybe worked with overseas embassies to glean data about your target market and the relevant players. As a part of this exercise, you can use historic trade show data to supplement or confirm the data you already have.

Previous trade show data will include lists of exhibitors and speakers. This will help you to understand the standing and influence of people who are prospective trade partners for you. You may also detect from photographs how these people present themselves and their brands. Could you see them representing you?

Historic exhibition data should also confirm who the major players are in the market. Some of these could be known to you but there may well be people of whom you have never heard. You may also pick up product varieties and modifications which are new to you.

## Visiting Exhibitions To Find Representatives

You can only find so much market research data from your desk. Visiting overseas exhibitions enables you to see for yourself the competitors, potential trade partners, product trends and market trends. As I mentioned earlier, your approach must be structured:-

*Objectives* – clarify why you are going and what you hope to get from the trip. What would be a good result?

*Method* – establish if you will go just as a visitor, or if you will book a modest exhibition stand. If you are taking a stand, what materials, props and products do you need? Do not forget brochures and some fact sheets in the local language. Business cards are essential. Check if your presence as an exhibitor attracts any funding.

*Preparation* – whether you are exhibiting or just visiting, get a stand guide as soon as you can, then make a list of all the stands you wish to visit. Arrange them in the order of a logical tour around the show. If you are exhibiting, arrive early and check all materials and exhibits work properly. Include prominent notification on your stand that you are seeking local representation.

*Travel & Appointments* – cities hosting exhibitions have a tendency towards full flights and full hotels around the time of the events, so it is important to book early. Or stay at nearby towns and travel on the days of the shows.

When you are exhibiting to try and attract potential partners, <u>don't just turn up and leave things to chance</u>. Contact likely prospects beforehand and invite them to your stand. Arrange specific appointments to avoid missing them. If prospective partners have their own stands, pay them a visit to see how they present themselves and the brands they represent. You need to arrange cover for those times when you are away from your stand. You can sometimes get bogged down talking with people who are clearly never going to work with you, so you must politely take all their details and move on. Exhibitions can be very gruelling, so make sure you have breakfast and keep yourself hydrated during the show. Avoid alcohol until after the show has closed each day.

*Following Up* – you may get everything right during your time at an exhibition but you can lose everything if you do not follow up effectively.

- Agree the meeting takeaways before concluding your discussions at the exhibition
- Send confirmation of all actions by email as soon as you get back to base (and avoid all distractions from colleagues who have been awaiting your return).
- Do whatever you have promised to do, without delay
- Maintain early enthusiasm levels
- Agree the next steps

I went to Copenhagen once for a first meeting with a prospective Danish distributor at a large multi-product exhibition, where he had a stand. I had difficulty in getting near to his stand because of the number of people attracted to the adjacent stand – it was someone demonstrating all the various benefits of South Sea oils on topless volunteers.

## Visiting Exhibitions To Support Your Representatives

I always found that my agents and distributors really appreciated the presence of their principal at exhibitions they were attending. They seem to enjoy "showing you off" to their customers and staff. Do not underestimate the value that your partners place upon your trade show support.

You ought to plan the exhibition (or at least your products' part in the exhibition) well in advance. If you are lucky with the timing, the show may be appropriate for you to unveil new products. Agree any cost-sharing, any display materials and any sample products. Arrange to meet the sales staff for a briefing before the show, especially if new products are being launched.

Set a good example by being punctual and smart. You should avoid the temptation to drink alcohol, even if others partake.

By supporting your representative at an exhibition, you can:-

- See how they present your products
- See how punctual, courteous and professional the sales team are
- Meet some of your representative's customers
- Meet your representative's other suppliers, as there may be some synergies. I found that representatives of certain other brands (portable appliances, televisions, audio systems, computers) often made a good fit for my products.

After a full day accompanying my Greek distributor at an exhibition in Thessaloniki, I was whisked up by car to Kilkis to attend the wedding reception of a retailer's daughter. When I arrived there, I was treated like royalty with the bride's father putting on a very dramatic dance for me. I just wanted the bride to be the centre of attention.

## Exhibiting Yourselves (Regionally or Globally)

At local or domestic shows, it is appropriate to support your representatives at their events but when it comes to large regional or global shows, you need to run the show yourselves. If a particular exhibition attracts visitors from lots of different countries, you cannot expect local representatives to answer all questions – and neither can local representatives be expected to pay for such events.

Organising your presence at large exhibitions requires military precision, planning and sheer hard work. Expect to have to start things off one year before the events take place. Here is a brief checklist of the kind of things you must consider:-

- Measurable objectives
- Stand size and layout
- Eye-catching design
- Display products
- Literature and translations
- Logistics
- Personal communications (paging etc)
- Travel and accommodation
- Funding and grants
- Invitations
- Support staff and interpreters
- Meeting rooms
- Refreshments
- There may be opportunities to get speaker slots at break-out sessions
- There should be a team briefing every morning, so that everyone knows who is expected to attend
- Similarly, a de-brief session at the end of each day will confirm how well, or otherwise, things are going.

It is important that your business is represented in a thoroughly professional way, so do not be afraid to bark out a few "house rules"

- Punctual arrival
- Smartness
- No alcohol before the exhibition closes each day
- No visitors to be left unattended
- All team members to assist with keeping the stand clean

Organising a presence at an overseas exhibition is extremely hard work, with dozens of things to get done by the start of each show. Working on an exhibition stand can be very tiring, so team members should be encouraged to wear comfortable footwear, keep themselves fed and hydrated and, if possible, avoid hangovers!

Working together as part of an exhibition team generates great camaraderie. Evans was the best I worked with at exhibitions, riding along on the crest of the exhibition wave until the stand was eventually broken down. He loved having a list of surplus products to shift and was always the first to congratulate his colleagues' good performances at the end-of-day de-briefing sessions.

Rather than use third party logistics, we used our own trucks and drivers to get stuff to exhibitions in Northern Europe. The drivers worked before and after the show but had time off during the show. We criticised them because they wasted their days in strip clubs. So, one day I gave them a long list of places to see in Paris (Louvre, Eiffel Tower, Sacre Coeur, Arc de Triomphe etc). When I caught them later in the day they confirmed that they had visited all the places I gave them – and then went to a strip club in the afternoon!

On that subject, I am reminded of the time two of my colleagues went for a walk after an exhibition in Frankfurt and they thought they had been invited to a local strip club. When they arrived, they were enthusiastically welcomed to a Christian Science meeting – not quite what they were expecting.

I managed to organise a Distributor Conference which ran for two days just before a Paris exhibition. As each distributor took to the stage for their presentation, our AV people played some typical music. The Greek, Irish and French bits went well, I just wish they hadn't played the theme from "The Dambusters" when our German people stepped up.

During one exhibition, my German colleague (who could often be a pain in the butt anyway) hammered on my hotel room door at 6.30am to see if I had a hair dryer he could borrow. Anyone less likely to have a hair dryer is difficult to imagine, since I resemble a billiard ball.

Often during exhibitions you get the chance to take your representatives out in the evening. My boss, Steven Marshall, and I took our Norwegian distributors out for a meal in Paris and after dinner drinks were ordered. I had been extolling the virtues of Irish whisky, so Jameson's and Black Bush were ordered all round. Only Steven and I saw the funny side when the waiter asked of the two blonde Norwegian ladies in our party, "whose is the Black Bush?"

Attending a show in Dubai resulted in a couple of memorable events. Firstly I was treated to a desert safari by jeep, which ended up with a Bedouin barbecue and a ride on a camel. The following evening our restaurant was entertained by a local belly dancer. She had Americans and Arabs reaching out for her – but who did she decide to make a beeline for? Yes, the reserved, pink-faced Brit at the back of the room.

I attended a seven day exhibition in Poznan, Poland, not too long after the Berlin Wall had come down. Getting decent food to eat was not easy but on the final evening the Kenwood distributor invited a number of us to his home, where he put on an excellent barbecue. Food was plentiful and I made a pig of myself. The following day at the exhibition, my gorging caught up with me, so I had to trot off to the smallest room. Unfortunately there was no loo paper in there, so I had to use the only thing available to me – Polish bank notes!

One night during an exhibition in Brno, Czech Republic, Evans and I were invited to sample some local wine, of which our distributor's brother was very proud. It was absolutely awful stuff but Evans and I demonstrated what good liars we were by complimenting our host. That resulted in them pouring more wine out for us but I seem to remember finding some convenient plant pots.

I attended a large exhibition at Storefjell, Norway, where there was a fine meal every evening and the diners were entertained by local comedians – in Norwegian of course. On the final evening one of the comedians unexpectedly reverted to English. He announced that there was someone English present, so he asked me to stand up while he told a joke in English. With all eyes on me, I simply had to laugh. Embarrassingly, it was a very anti-German joke which he thought I would appreciate.

During a three day exhibition in Utrecht, Netherlands, I was intrigued as to why some of the men disappeared for a while. I was soon shown why! My host took me for a walk down the waterway to where the Utrecht "boat women" resided. They advertised their services with the curtains open and then closed the curtains when a client arrived.

# 11. IRELAND

The English will say it is serious, but not a disaster. The Irish will tell you it is a disaster …. ah but it's not serious. (Anon)

I am not so think as you drunk I am. (Sir John Collings Squire)

Ireland is an island which is 300 miles long and 170 miles thick. (Niall Toibin)

When I worked as an adviser to new British exporters, unless there were obvious climatic factors suggesting the contrary, I told them to look closely at the Republic of Ireland. I know that it only has 5 million inhabitants but there are many reasons why the Irish market is attractive:-

- It is physically very close to the U.K.
- There are well-established air and sea links
- They speak English
- It is a reasonably affluent country
- With a relatively young population, the Irish are open to new ideas
- The Irish people are extremely good hosts, they are great conversationalists and they have a terrific sense of humour

When I first started handling the Irish market, I inherited a piece of business worth less than a million pounds a year. By the time I handed it over, the market was worth 11 million pounds a year to us – so we clearly did something right there!

A marketing consultant named Alastair Campbell (no, not that one!) once said to me that the four most important words in marketing are "Listen To Your Customers" – and that is what I did in the Irish market. When I asked my distributors in Dublin how we could serve the Irish market better they said we should change three things:-

1. Visit the market more often
2. Stop treating Ireland as merely a British afterthought
3. Make commercial decisions based upon local market conditions

Americans often refer to "the European market" but there really is no such thing. I discovered over the years that Spanish markets are not like Portuguese markets, the Dutch and Belgian markets have different players and different dynamics. Similarly, the Irish market is not the same as the British market and the Irish get annoyed when British sales staff just waltz in and fail to recognise the differences.

Although the vast majority of Irish are very positive towards the British, you need to understand why some of them may not be. Take the trouble to read up on Irish history – go way back to Brian Ború in the 11th century, learn about Wolfe Tone's activities and understand why Oliver Cromwell didn't make the British over-popular in Ireland. Realise why Britain's lack of support during the Great Potato Famine has not been forgotten and don't forget that many Irish folks nowadays had grandparents who were involved in the events between 1916 and 1922. The "Troubles" in the North are still fairly recent, so my advice is not to pass comment on those issues (nor any religious differences), but at least try to understand why some of the Irish might feel the way they do.

The problem when you are travelling the world with a British passport is that you are often "blamed" for some of our colonial legacies and it is fair to say that we don't exactly have an unblotted copybook when it comes to Ireland.

I visited the Republic of Ireland pretty much every month over eleven years and I got to know them better than they knew themselves. My boss once said "Mike, you have become more Irish than the Irish themselves". I don't think it was intended as a compliment, but I took it as such!

The biggest mistake made by British business people is that they underestimate the Irish. Too many people still go along with the insulting old 1960s and 1970s comedians' archetype of the stupid, thick Irishman. Believe me, nothing could be further from the truth. They are very cute in their negotiations and I have seen a number of Brits over the years almost have their trousers taken down by smart "Paddies".

Ireland has a young, well-educated workforce. They are not backwards at coming forwards, they are stimulating, challenging and creative. In terms of logistics, communications and technology, Ireland is well-developed and has good relationships with the U.K., the U.S.A. and the European Community. British television is watched in the Republic, so they are familiar with current events in Britain.

I believe that I have been to, or through, all 26 counties of the Republic. I mentioned elsewhere in this book that, to understand a market, you must know your customers' customers. I did just that in Ireland, regularly visiting large retailers in Dublin as well as tiny little stores in rural areas.

Without picking up many of the local Irish language words, I did learn a few new collective nouns – "skelp", "skite", "clatter" and "rake" for example. And there were a few descriptions of people that I had not heard before – "hooer", "fecker", "eejit", "gurrier" and "nacker" all come to mind. In some parts of Ireland, I played my "Welshness" card, as Taffies were more acceptable in areas like West Cork.

Over these years I was able to build a stronger, closer relationship with my distributor's staff than any of our competitors could manage. We became market leaders in Ireland, occasionally even attaining higher market shares than in the U.K. This was my greatest success during my time in export and I became extremely fond of the great characters I worked with.

My chief collaborator within my distributor's staff was Oliver Edwards, a great guy to work with and also genuinely funny. He could put on any of the local Irish accents, very accurately and very hilariously. Oliver attended a distributor conference in Madrid on one occasion and was soon in full flow, telling jokes to the other delegates. One of our number, poor Vic Alcott, laughed so much that he choked quite violently and had to be rushed to hospital.

Oliver and I spent a full week, driving around Ireland in a Hiace van (like a couple of "nackers" according to our colleagues) as we delivered a series of presentations to local retail staff. The van was necessary as we were showing bulky components and products. One of the places we visited was in County Roscommon and we believe that it contained the biggest family in Ireland – based upon the number of claim forms we received for free dinnerware sets!

At a dinner with a team of Irish sales representatives, Oliver continually teased the Cork rep, Dennis Owens, in a remarkably accurate and funny Cork accent. Dennis smiled but was clearly getting fed up with the remorseless micky-taking. So, he stood up and addressed me. "Young man, you are very welcome in Ireland – but not all British visitors were welcome in Ireland. The worst visitor from Britain was a man called Oliver Cromwell. He was a nasty piece of work, he was an absolute bastard. And we have never forgotten him to this day – in fact, the biggest bastards in Ireland are still called Oliver."

I mentioned that I had seen all 26 counties. During one journey in the late 1980s my Training Manager was driving us from Monaghan to Dundalk on a concessionary road through part of Northern Ireland. Around one corner, we were stopped and were confronted by men in camouflage gear, brandishing guns. Thankfully they were British troops, who checked our ID and waived us through. That was a really scary moment, though.

The Irish like to pop for a pint after work and I was only too happy to go along with that practice. On one occasion, I joined Oliver at 5pm in Ryans of Parkgate Street and one

Guinness followed another, and then another – followed by a bite to eat. I eventually reached my hotel at 2am!

One of the Dublin pubs I was taken to was "Dockers", which was often used by the band members of U2, as it was close to their recording studio. I asked if the band were mobbed when they came in. "Oh no" came the reply, "we wouldn't give them the satisfaction of being recognised!" There is a wonderful irreverence about the Irish, they do not respect reputations.

Trade shows in Ireland often go on until late at night and the rule seems to be that the bar will remain open until the last customer leaves. At a show in Galway, one customer was the last to leave and was clearly the worse for wear. As he got up to leave, he was asked "Paddy, will ye not have one for the ditch?"

There is a comic couple in the "Father Ted" series called John and Mary. They appear to be very loving in front of other folks but they resort to brawling as soon as they are left alone. I reckon that I must have had the room next to a similarly aggressive couple at Malahide one night, although there was little evidence of it in the breakfast room the following day.

One of our retailers put on a weekend event for some of their selected sales staff at Clifden, west of Galway (very close to where Alcock and Brown landed after their transatlantic flight) – and I was invited to join them, probably because we were paying for some of it. My main memory of the weekend was taking part in a treasure hunt around Connemara on the second day with a sore head!

Sometimes it was my turn to play the part of the host and one year this involved taking a group of Irish retailers to see

"Miss Saigon" in London, followed by a meal and further drinks back at our hotel. Unfortunately, Oliver cut his head on the door leading into the gents loo, and spent the rest of the evening looking like Mikhail Gorbachev!

I have mentioned some of the good times to be had when doing business with the Irish but there is a serious point here. If all other factors are equal, I usually advise most new exporters to cut their teeth in markets which are close in proximity, relatively affluent, similar business culture to the U.K., and speak good English. This usually narrows down to three areas – Benelux, Scandinavia and Ireland. So, before tackling bigger or more ambitious markets, take a good look at the Republic of Ireland – but make sure you take an umbrella. Why do you think it is so green?

# 12. THE U.S.A.

I am not the smartest fellow in the world, but I can sure pick smart colleagues (Franklin D. Roosevelt)

The road to success is always under construction (Lily Tomlin)

Our greatest glory is not in never failing, but in rising up every time we fail (Ralph Waldo Emerson)

When compiling this book, I felt that doing business with the U.S.A. justified a chapter all of its own, not least because it represents one of the mistakes that British exporters make more than any other. We mistakenly assume that dealing with Americans will be exactly the same as dealing with the British – after all, we speak the same language, watch each other's films and listen to each other's music. Having made that assumption, we then dive into situations without understanding why things might be different. And then we get our fingers burned!

You need to consider what the Americans and British think of each other – and why. Then you need to understand why and how we are different. And then you need to realise what you must do differently if you are to be successful in your dealings with the U.S.A.

## What do we think of Americans?

Impatient – we think that Americans are in a hurry, always seeking to move on without indulging in "small talk".

Brash, Rude, Impolite – taking impatience one stage further, we think that Americans can be less than courteous – even offensive on occasions.

Straight-talking – Americans are not known for being very diplomatic. They get to the point and don't mince their words. And they expect the same in response. I stumbled into a product training session in Dublin once, delivered by an American colleague, Dennis Welch. He claimed that the best feature of his American-built washing machine was that "it sure gets rid of skid marks".

Loud – an American once told me that he had been living in England long enough to stop speaking on trains. Americans seem not to have a volume control. I once sat on a plane just in front of a gentleman who was employed by one of our competitors. By the time we reached Cincinnati, I knew all their marketing plans for the next six months!

Technically competent – we expect that Americans will be up to date with the very latest gadgets, systems and buzz words. But don't expect them to know anything about metric measurements.

Decisive – we expect Americans to avoid "beating about the bush". We believe that they will make their minds up quickly and press on with an action plan.

Competitive and Driven – we know that Americans like to win and that their losers are quickly forgotten.

Self-confident – even from a young age, Americans appear to be articulate, confident speakers. Their positivity was illustrated by a phrase I picked up in Kentucky – "God willing and the creek don't rise".

Open – we know Americans to be frank and not afraid to get to the bottom of things. We don't expect them to keep information to themselves.

Reliable – after years of collaboration on the international stage, we know that Americans do what they say they will do. We are confident they will make good trading partners.

Pro-British – generally speaking, Americans are very positive towards British people and they extend this to our goods and services. As a result, we expect to be received with warmth and co-operation.

Ignorant of anything not American – surprisingly, only a relatively small percentage of Americans have passports. As a result, they can be insular and not as knowledgeable about foreign countries as might be expected.

The above points are not exactly factual, more a series of perceptions. They are what we think, for whatever reason. By the same token, Americans have their own perceptions about British people and businesses.

**What do Americans think of us?**

Reserved – they think we are slow to open up, that we are shy and that we definitely don't talk on trains! They therefore conclude that perhaps we are not overly-confident in our goods and services.

Reliable – after many years of working together in commerce as well as in politics, Americans think that the British are good partners who always deliver what was promised.

Honest – Americans regard the British to be as honest as just about any people on the planet. This is a great starting point when you are looking to create new business partnerships.

Polite and courteous – they expect us to have good manners, both personal and commercial.

Predictable – Americans do not expect us to surprise them. They think they know what to expect from us.

Risk-averse – they think we are not prepared to take chances, that we will always choose the "safe" option.

Traditional – with many centuries of history behind us, we are expected to be trapped in the past. Despite our recent track record on innovation, we are still regarded as traditionalists.

Resistant to change – because of the perception that we are risk-averse and traditional, Americans think that we are slow to accept change.

So, we have lists of differences, either perceived or actual. It is important to understand why we are different, and how this has affected the way in which we do business.

**Why are Americans different?**

In 1620, the "Mayflower" set sail from England and the first English settlers (the Pilgrims) arrived in New England. This was an extremely bold move by a group of people who took a gamble and made a fresh start.

Between 1848 and 1855 America experienced a "Gold Rush", especially in California, where lots of people from inside and outside the U.S.A. joined the westerly movement in order to seek their fortune. Again, these folks took a gamble and made a fresh start.

Between 1892 and 1914 large numbers of people left Europe and moved to the U.S.A. These were mostly Jews, escaping persecution, and Italians, escaping poverty. These immigrants went through a large clearing station on Ellis Island, as many as 1900 a day at its peak. Something like 40% of Americans claim that at least one of their parents descended from the Ellis Island processing station. And, once again, these immigrants took a gamble and made a fresh start.

So, of course Americans are impatient, driven and self-confident. They are the descendants of pioneers, decision makers and risk takers. Just think about it – the people who cosily stayed behind and waved off the "Mayflower" are the ancestors of current British business owners.

Having looked at why Americans are different, these impact upon the way in which Americans go about running their businesses.

## How are Americans different?

Time – The U.S.A. is rich in resources but they recognise that the only resource which is not plentiful is time. The Americans like to push on and they don't like anything which wastes their time. The phrase "time is money" is typical of the U.S.A.

Pleasantries – when making telephone calls or starting meetings, Americans like to get straight on with business. Unlike many other cultures, they don't want to talk about families, sport or the weather, at least not until the business conversation has ended.

Informality – Americans like to use first names from the outset. Similarly, business attire has become far more relaxed in recent years.

Deal-focused – having said that Americans avoid the wasting of time at the beginning of discussions, they like to drive meetings forward with a view to the achieving of a favourable outcome in the shortest of time. They will invariably interrupt presentations, rather than save questions until the end. They have a very obvious "can do" attitude.

Regional differences – the above points are generalisations but it cannot be ignored that there are regional variations, as you would expect in such a large country. There is something of a north-south divide, with Southerners being less time-conscious than Northerners. Easterners tend to be more formal than people based in the West.

Some business practices are now becoming more influenced by those in Latin America, as the Hispanic population continues to grow.

Own experiences – there is no doubt that I developed significantly as a result of working with Americans. After the "blame culture" which I experienced in the U.K. in the 1970s and 1980s, it was a refreshing change to encounter the American approach to mistakes. The priority was what had been learned from the experience, not whose fault it had been. Obviously the repetition of mistakes was asking for trouble, though.

I always found Americans to be fair, motivated and positive. They were actually easy when it came to the presentation of new products, because they wanted to be impressed. Sales training sessions were a pleasure, as the Americans just swallowed up the features and benefits.

Americans make great team colleagues, as there is always lots of mutual praise, back-slapping and high fives.

One of the most powerful business tools I learned from Americans was something called Quick Market Intelligence (QMI). This consisted of the gathering together of perhaps 10 or 12 actual customers in a hotel or business centre between 7pm and 9pm with a view to collecting immediate market feedback. Market trends, competitive activity, what you are doing well and what you are doing badly were all discussed, and it was agreed what actions should be taken. The following morning, the actions were fed back by video call to the senior directors.

Once the business discussions are finished, Americans can be generous and convivial hosts. I was once treated to a meal on a floating restaurant which sailed gently up the Ohio River from Louisville, and then back again. Unfortunately, our trip was curtailed when the captain saw the size of the storm rapidly approaching us. We swiftly turned round and completed our journey, almost at a pace suitable for water skiing!

Having picked up on the different ways in which Americans do business, you must consider what you will do differently as a result. The way they do business is not wrong, but you will have to change the way you work if you are to successfully build business relationships with them.

**What must you do differently?**

*Regionalisation* – you should give strong consideration to the handling of the market on a regional basis. Many American organisations say that they can handle the whole of the country but they are usually only strong in their own region. To handle the whole of the U.S.A. satisfactorily, you will probably need 5 or 6 partners.

*Legal Issues* – you must be aware that U.S.A. business is very litigious, caused mainly by the fact that the loser does not have to pay the winner's costs. In most cases the potential winner will try to string things out so that the potential loser's costs could reach alarming levels. The potential winner then offers to settle out of court for a sum far less than the potential loser's costs.

U.K. contracts may not apply in the U.S.A. – so do not assume that U.S.A. law will be the same as English law. If you decide to set up a U.S.A. subsidiary, you must ensure that your subsidiary is a separate entity otherwise the British parent company could become involved in any American litigation.

Product liability is a potential nightmare, so you must take advice. Before committing to U.S.A. market entry, make sure that you identify all legal, insurance and Intellectual Property costs. You should also check registration, compliance and accreditation.

*Presentations* – at meetings, cut out all your usual pleasantries and just dive straight into the business chat. Make sure your presentations are brisk and factual. Avoid using British idioms and sayings, as they will not be understood by Americans. Check all your props beforehand, as wasted time will not be well-received. The advice I received was "in General Electric, it doesn't matter how good you are. What counts is how good your charts are".

*Negotiations* – try to avoid blatantly saying "no" to their suggestions, saying that you will investigate and then get back to them. Be seen as a creative and flexible negotiator, so have lots of alternatives up your sleeve.

*Marketing* – be prepared to re-write all marketing text. Brochures, leaflets, advertising, websites etc. must all be scrutinised and changed. Be bold and do what the Americans do, so use superlatives (biggest, fastest-growing, most innovative) and words which express confidence (guarantee, promise, assure).

*Sport* – Americans are great lovers of sport and you can score a few points for yourself by taking an interest in American Football and Baseball. If you fancy a challenge, you can do what I did one evening. Over dinner, my American guest asked me to explain the laws of cricket to him. Two hours later, he said cheerio with his head spinning!

My colleague and friend, Nigel Truswell, once accompanied me to the U.S.A. and the blighter discovered (not for the first time) that he had managed to travel without any cash. It is not difficult to guess who picked up all the bills for taxis and food on that trip! By the way, Nigel introduced me to the work of John Shuttleworth, for which I will always be grateful. Oof!

This all sounds like an awful lot to take on board and some businesses will ask whether it is all worth it. But I certainly am not trying to scare you away from the American market. This is a big, exciting, dynamic market and the opportunities are immense – but you simply must prepare thoroughly so that you avoid the many pitfalls. Working with such positive and lively people in such a vibrant marketplace can be very stimulating, so your earlier hard work will pay off.

# 13. MANAGING OVERSEAS TRADING PARTNERS

The best executive is one who has sense enough to pick good people to do what he wants done, and then self-restraint enough to keep from meddling with them while they are doing it. (Theodore Roosevelt)

Some countries drive on the left. Some countries drive on the right. In Malta, we drive in the shade. (Adrian Busietta)

Writing advertisements is the second most profitable form of writing. The first, of course, is ransom notes. (Philip Dusenberry)

Over the years, I have been confronted many times by exporters who blame their lack of export growth on two factors:-

1. "We need to enter new markets"
2. "Our representatives are under-performing".

After analysing the situation, I concluded in almost every case that they <u>didn't</u> need new export markets and their representatives were <u>not</u> under-performing. The problem existed because they themselves were not doing a proper job in their existing markets. If your exports are not growing as you wish, then it is <u>almost certainly your own fault</u>!

When you appoint new overseas trading partners, you will quite rightly be very pleased and relieved. But that is not the point where the hard work ends, it is the point where the real hard work begins.

Start off on the right foot. Although the newly-created trading partnership has been set up for mutual benefit, it is important that you set the tone and drive the relationship. This will not always be easy, as your representatives will often be strong-willed and in some cases will be the heads of fairly large organisations. You should respect their positions, of course, but no matter how they run their own businesses, it has to be you driving the partnership.

It is vital that you build mutual trust with your local representative and you should both sign an Agreement such as the one suggested in chapter 8. This will ensure that both parties are aware of their own and their partners' duties and responsibilities.

As well as signing an Agreement, the parties must agree to a set of Key Performance Indicators (KPIs). Measurable KPIs should be achievable, realistic and time-bound. These could be such things as:-

- Sales results, by product group or model
- Sales results by geographical region
- Sales results by distribution channel or by customer
- Market share percentages by business sector
- Numbers of new customers
- Product availability measures
- Stockholding and stock turns
- Speed of after sales service
- Customer and consumer satisfaction levels

The setting of such performance-monitoring data will ensure that the partnership thrives in a manageable way. The KPIs should be reviewed regularly and the results should be acted upon.

If things are not progressing as planned, you will obviously want to meet with your trading partner to establish what can be done. But before that meeting, you need to take a good look at your own performance, to see what you could be doing differently. As I said earlier, there is a very good chance that it is your fault, not theirs.

**Firstly, review the Four Ps:-**

*Product* – is your offering consistent with what the export market requires? Are there any size, format, colour or material issues? Have you catered for local language issues? Do you comply with local standards and regulations? Is there any customisation you should consider? In other words, are you supplying something which is just too difficult for your local partner to sell?

*Price* – is the final price to the end consumer fair and competitive? Have you built all of the cost adders into your pricing calculation? Who is taking the exchange rate risk? Are all margins within the supply chain acceptable? Are all sales staff being sufficiently incentivised?

*Place* – is your chosen route to market the most appropriate for that country? Have you conceded exclusivity? Is your trading partner located in the right place? What additional training or support can you give?
As a very last resort, does your partner need to be changed?

*Promotion* – Have you reminded yourself why you are exporting? Who is responsible for each element within the budget for promotional activity (manufacturer, distributor, reseller, retailer)? Is the expenditure by both parties adequate? Is the mix of activities right (traditional, social, media, press)? Are the positioning of the product and the positioning of the price supported by appropriate promotional activity?

To coincide with a visit by my boss and I, one of our distributors sponsored a local "beauty contest" – it was the 1980s, after all. When asked if we could supply a member of the panel to judge the bikini-clad young ladies, I suggested that my boss' seniority should come into play. He got the job, thankfully.

The next time I visited that particular location, we experienced a minor earthquake, so never a dull moment!

Talking of beauty contests, reminds me of two other incidents. My Maltese distributor sponsored a contestant in the 1984 Maltese heat of "Miss World" – and she won, so she came to London (as "Miss Malta") for the actual "Miss World" final. The day after the contest, all of the contestants were taken out by their respective sponsors for promotional activity, photo shoots etc. So I was given the job of collecting Miss Malta from a hotel foyer (where all of the contestants were meeting their sponsors) and taking her back to our showroom. She was very pleasant and became a TV presenter in later years.

Linda Pétursdóttir was the Icelandic contestant in the 1988 "Miss World" event and won the title. Some time afterwards, I caught a really early morning flight back from Keflavik and Miss World was sat next to me. As it was dreadfully early, we fell asleep on the journey. So I suppose I can say that I slept with Miss World! I bet she mentions it to all her friends.

**Secondly, discuss the KPIs with your representative:-**

- Share your vision, your plans and your aspirations
- Review the data together, identifying what has gone wrong in a blame-free, constructive way
- Discuss your own analysis of the Four Ps and how they may have to be modified
- Understand what has changed since your previous discussions – the economic climate, the political situation, competitive actions etc
- Together, draw up an agreed list of issues, problems, shortfalls

Whilst discussing issues with local representatives, some of them took the opportunity to show me examples of problem products in consumers' homes. I therefore had the pleasure of being confronted by irate customers in the basements of their homes – everywhere from Reykjavik to Buenos Aires!

**Thirdly, agree actions with which to drive forwards:-**

What additional support must you provide (sales training, technical training, customer care training, trade show support, more virtual meetings, accompaniment of representative's sales staff)?

What must your representative do differently (staff training, staff incentives, customer training, local trade shows, local advertising, sponsorship, U.K. visits)?

Should both parties communicate more regularly or in different ways? Should other members of staff communicate more often to enable the sharing of best practices?

One of the challenges facing exporters is to ensure that your products and brand receive a fair percentage of your representative's time and resources. Of course, they have other items in their portfolio and, whilst you must respect that, you must also push for a fair share. My Greek distributor was very active in the "brown goods" sector – televisions, video and audio items. I arrived in Athens one evening and he proudly told me that he had supplied my hotel with over 100 Romanian television sets, one for each room. When I went to my room, I turned on the television, which seemed fine. But then, after my shower, I pressed the top of my deodorant can – and the television changed channel!

**Fourthly, agree new KPIs to get back on track:-**

In the light of your discussions, some of the KPIs may need tweaking. Your role here is to find the happy medium between keeping your representative energised and ensuring you are both continuing to work towards a positive and mutually-profitable outcome.

A number of exporters clearly underestimate the amount of effort needed to support new overseas representatives. There is much hand-holding to be done, most of which cannot be done from behind a desk in the U.K. Regular visits are necessary (a) to develop the relationship and (b) to deliver the plan.

You have to set the tone, take the lead and drive the relationship. We are talking about your products, your brand and your reputation.

**Don't let the tail wag the dog!**

When travelling out for progress meetings with my overseas representatives, I had some interesting flights. After returning from Dublin once, I received a call from Ryanair telling me to report to my doctor immediately as the passenger sitting next to me had gone down with a strain of meningitis.

On another occasion I was one of only two passengers on an SAS flight from Copenhagen. It was the day after Saddam Hussein had threatened to shoot down Western passenger planes and all the other passengers had cancelled. We had excellent service though!

I used to try and support my Maltese distributor by attending the annual Trade Fair. It was a good opportunity to see how they presented our products and to see the competition as well. On one occasion I picked up the "Maltese Times" on the plane and read on the front page that I was one of the Fair's expected notable visitors!

I took my new colleague, Sarah Dudley, to meet our Belgian distributor, who took us out to lunch after our meeting. Somehow, Sarah managed to squirt curry sauce down her immaculate white blouse. As we left the restaurant, she whispered to me "classy bird, aren't I?"

In fairness, Sarah was one of the best-organised colleagues I worked with – she worked with me at Hotpoint and again when we had both become advisers. She didn't just squirt sauce on herself!

Getting your overseas representatives to visit you in the UK is another good example of building close relationships. One of my factory directors used to take great pride in flying the customers' flags when they arrived, and this gave the customers much pleasure – apart from the time when we used the flag of the "wrong" Cyprus, and apart from the time when we flew the German flag upside down!

During a visit by some General Electric distributors to the U.K., they requested that they be taken on a traditional English pub night out. So, a fish and chip restaurant was booked and they were later taken on a mini pub crawl around the centre of Chester. We finished up by teaching them to play darts and snooker. We were very impressed at the speed with which the Russians picked up snooker. Their engineering and mathematical minds enabled them to work out angles so accurately.

**Sharing of Best Practices**

When you enter new markets, your ultimate aim should be for your activity in the new markets to be as successful as in the U.K. Now, although it may have taken you many years to establish yourselves in the U.K., it doesn't necessarily have to take you as long to get established in your new markets. This is because your new activity can learn from the experiences and mistakes you have made in your domestic market. This sharing of best practices is vital if you are to mirror your activity in your new markets.

Whenever possible, I tried to accompany my overseas representatives' sales staff on customer visits – partly to meet their retailers, partly to see how our products were being presented, and partly to see what our competitors were up to. You cannot always rely on what you are told, as many things are said with an agenda behind them. Go and see for yourselves.

There are a number of areas where you can "teach" your overseas trading partners how to develop and grow your brand in their local markets. This can include ideas on:-

- Promotions, advertising, sponsorship
- Staff incentives and rewards
- Sales force organisation and motivation
- Sales forecasting
- Stock management and Requirements Planning
- Warranty and servicing offers

You will need to spend a lot of time with your trading partners, making plenty of visits. This is why I always advise new exporters not to take on too many new markets at once. It is better to give good quality support to a small number of markets, rather than "scattergun" the world and do a poor job in lots of markets.

By helping to make your trading partners' businesses to be more successful and profitable, they will react by putting more time and effort into the growth of your brand and products. **Win-Win!**

I was very lucky in that I was supported by some outstanding colleagues. By introducing such colleagues to my distributors, I was able to share best practices at a really effective level.

I had the resources of a sales training team which was the "best in class", an absolutely outstanding team managed by Glenys Gray – who was the most professional and polished person I ever worked with. Glenys established very high standards for herself and her team, and she never allowed those standards to drop. Her team were always punctual, vivacious, smart and well-prepared.

One of Glenys' team was Christine Knott, who would have made a good stand-up comic. Christine came to Malta with me on one occasion to train the local sales team. I had a meeting with the directors while Christine trained the team. Upon my return, as I approached the training room, all I could hear was raucous laughter. Christine believed that all trainees should enjoy themselves while they were learning.

Bob Wardell was a very experienced technician blessed with a wicked Scouse sense of humour. He went with me to Sydney in order to train the local Australian service engineers on a range of new products. I attended a couple of hours of one of his sessions and I was able to witness how Bob could vary his delivery between very correct technical terms and the more "industrial" language which was occasionally called for!

I once took one of our quality inspectors on a trip to the Mediterranean. He was a capable enough individual but he had no idea how to travel. On a long journey there are times to talk, times to shut up, times to read and times to sleep. Unfortunately, my colleague felt obliged to talk all the way there and all the way back. I felt like jumping out of the emergency exit at times!

 Andrew Lillywhite was a most capable packaging engineer, who later made a career in logistics management. He and another colleague came with me to Athens to advise the local distributor on product handling issues. On the final evening at our hotel, they introduced me to the "Round the Optics" game in the bar. Let's just say that I slept pretty well after that.

Andrew also came with me to Dublin once and we experienced a 6 hour flight delay. After we had parked up, the IRA lobbed a mortar bomb (over the top of our parked car) onto the runway at Heathrow. On those occasions, it is the lack of information which is the frustration. If you are told how long your delay will be, you can manage the situation. But not knowing is awful.

**Outside Help**

During your meetings and conversations with your overseas representatives, you will detect certain levels of satisfaction and comfort within your partner. But they may not open up to you – which can result in their suffering in silence. There may be things about which they are unhappy, but they don't feel able to talk with you about it. If you are brave enough, you could get a third party consultant to talk with your representatives about the relationship and their support from you. Your partner needs to be fully on board with you, so make sure you identify and address any issues they may have.

**Building an Export Sales Team**

I have talked here about managing overseas partners, with the intention of growing the business and then repeating the model in other markets. I mentioned the need to be excellent in a small number of markets but if you continue to be excellent, then logically you will want to enter new markets and build a network of representatives. But, of course, you cannot look after all of those activities yourself. If you are to manage a growing number of partners, then you are going to have to recruit a team of people to support you. In the early days, the export support will come from people who just absorb the work into their normal jobs. But as volumes grow, you will need to create a team specialising in export business. So, what is the bare minimum you will need?

**Marketing and Administration** – you will need someone who can take the exploratory enquiries and they must act as a focal point for correspondence with your appointed representatives. If you are lucky, such people will be linguists – but the priority is for them to be well-organised, courteous and motivated. Depending upon your route to market, you may need someone to create and monitor sales literature – plus the ability to organise travel plans.

**Shipping** – you could outsource all of your shipping and documentation work but, even if you do so initially, you should constantly review whether or not you should take it in-house. You then have to decide whether to train your existing staff or recruit ready-trained external staff. Export shipping is not the same as domestic logistics and you will need the right type of people to cope with it.

**Finance** – achieving export sales will expose your business to different terms of sale, different currencies and different terms of payment. Again, you have to consider whether to train or to recruit.

**Technical** – depending upon how complex your products are, you may choose to use U.K. staff as technical support, or you could just use one dedicated individual for all export liaison and support.

**Sales** – now we get to the real challenge! You will need to build a team of salespeople who can take the load off your shoulders, a team of self-motivated professionals who have good business acumen and plenty of stamina.

You can organise the team on things like geography, type of business or product group. It is important to get the right "horses for courses", as some parts of the world require different language skills and experience of handling certain cultures.

If I may be controversial here, I always found it easier to mould a bright U.K. salesperson into an effective export salesperson, than to take a linguist and teach them how to sell. The worst export sales people I encountered were linguists with MBAs. They developed very warm and cosy relationships with their customers, but then missed every sales target.

I said earlier that you don't have to use the same route to market across the world. Rather than employ a sales person to handle a particular region of the world, you could look at appointing an experienced self-employed sales agent to handle any resellers or distributors in the region. Of course, the agent will need to be paid a commission, but the model might just work more effectively than by employing someone.

If you recruit the right export sales team, they should be pushing back and challenging you with new ideas which they have learned from their travels. This can be a very stimulating environment in which to work.

## Conferences

As a method of sharing best practices and a way to get good quality feedback, you could organise a conference for your trading partners – preferably to coincide with a large event, like an exhibition which most delegates would have been attending anyway. It needs to be somewhere with good transport links.

Conferences are not cheap, as they will almost certainly involve you in hotel and meal expenses. You cannot put up delegates in a seedy backstreet hotel and neither can you take them round the corner to the local burger bar. The location and its environment both need to be pleasant, with all the facilities you would expect when travelling abroad on business. Be careful, however, not to get caught with delegates' bar bills outside of meal times.

When planning the itinerary, you should strive to include the following:-

- Presentations on your own business, your export progress and any likely future investments
- Case study reports delivered by a couple of the delegates
- New product presentations
- Facilitated round-table discussions on products
- Facilitated round-table discussions on support and training
- Both round-table sessions should generate action points
- A trip to a local place of interest
- Sociable activities, maybe even a golf tournament
- You should make up a "goodie pack", with things like baseball caps, laptop bags, sweatshirts, information folders, pens and mousemats.
- Try to follow up after a conference by encouraging your various representatives to stay in touch with each other. You could organise online conference calls to facilitate the sharing of best practices.

# 14. SUPPORT FOR EXPORTERS

You must learn from the mistakes of others. You can't possibly live long enough to make them all yourself. (Sam Levenson)

Behind every great man is a woman rolling her eyes. (Jim Carrey)

All wisdom is not new wisdom. (Winston Churchill)

Moving into a big new world of exporting may seem a little daunting but there is actually plenty of support available. The amount of support and the financial resources can vary across the U.K. but, in principle, the following sources of support are pretty much available to all British exporters.

As "rookie" exporters, do not be afraid to ask for advice. Someone has the answer to all your questions, someone else has already experienced what you are going through and someone will know a third party who can help you.

Do not dive into overseas situations based just upon your U.K. experiences. I have already mentioned the importance of doing your research, and this includes finding out what help is available. This list is not exhaustive, but it is a good place to start:-

**Department for Business and Trade (DBT)**, previously known as the DIT and UKTI, and no doubt to experience further name changes going forward.

When I was looking at new markets back in the late 1980s, I used the services of what was then called the British Overseas Trade Board (BOTB). This was then re-named Trade Partners, which used to pick up some wife-swapping sites when fed into search engines! But, whatever the departments have been called over the years, the British Government has always provided help for businesses looking to export British goods and services.

All would-be exporters must contact the DBT as early in the game as possible, in order to understand the range of services available. Fully-funded and match-funded services include:-

- Free support from a large team of locally-based International Trade Advisers

- Online and face-to-face training on a wide range of export-related topics
- Modest funding to support "internationalisation" costs, like translation work
- Modest funding to support travel expenses
- Modest funding to support overseas exhibiting expenses
- Accompanied market visits
- Assessment of your website
- Country guides
- Market research (chargeable)
- Use of overseas embassies (chargeable) for special events like product launches

Many new exporters approach the DBT purely looking for grants and subsidies. But it is not money that you need, it is knowledge and advice. And that is exactly what DBT has in abundance. You shouldn't be exporting purely because you have heard that grants are available. Your decision to export should stand up on its own, unsupported by other factors. Any monies you receive thereafter should just be a bonus. If a matched funded amount of only £2000 makes all the difference, then you probably shouldn't be exporting at all.

**HMRC**

A common misconception amongst international traders is that HMRC exists purely to catch you out when you have done something wrong. This is completely untrue – the department exists to help you to get things right in the first place. As a result, you should have no qualms about contacting HMRC for advice.

Before speaking with the people at HMRC, I recommend that you read up on the relevant website page first, to understand some of the terminology used by them. Make sure you understand the various Incoterms and take the trouble to read up on Rules of Origin. Finally, make sure that you understand all VAT implications, both when trading with the EU and with the rest of the world.

If you cannot find the answers and advice online, then contact HMRC. If you are not sure, do not guess, as it could be costly.

## Institute of Export and International Trade

The IOE delivers detailed training for people looking for a professional qualification in international trade. I recommend that all full-time Shipping Managers or Supervisors follow this route. If a business is exporting (or importing) large numbers of shipments involving a variety of countries, it makes sense to employ suitably-qualified specialists.

But the IOE is more than just that. They regularly deliver topical presentations on a variety of subjects, using experts in their fields. Their daily updates make for interesting and useful reading. They also offer facilities for members to ask questions of each other – a real messageboard with which to contact other exporting professionals. There is no need to repeat other people's mistakes.

## Chambers of Commerce

Every exporter should become a member of the local Chamber of Commerce. The Chambers provide a number of services for exporters, particularly dealing with special documents and processes.

They also put on events, with guest speakers and visiting authorities on overseas markets. Not to be missed are their half-day and full-day training courses on various aspects of exporting, especially Letters Of Credit, Incoterms and Commodity Codes. These are not the detailed courses offered by the IOE but they are ideal for export sales staff looking to glean more information on processes and documents.

The other members of the Chamber can be very useful. These include other exporters, intermediaries and providers of export services.

**Carriers**

When you start in exporting, you will soon realise that your best friends are your carriers. They will get you out of trouble when you have made mistakes. Their sole purpose is to ensure that your items get from your premises to your customers' premises quickly and without snags. They will check therefore that all your documentation is present and correct, often asking questions if they think something has been omitted.

By using the term "Carriers", I am including shipping companies, freight forwarders, hauliers, couriers, logistics providers and transport companies. Whichever type of carrier you use, be pedantic and check with them exactly what they are going to do and which documents they are going to provide. Most importantly, confirm the situation regarding the lodging of Customs Declarations.

If you are making a shipment to the EU, your carrier will need to know who is paying the import VAT, and whether the Postponed scheme is being used.

As with all suppliers of services, you should shop around for freight rates, whilst recognising the value of their advice and support.

## Suppliers

I was always told that you should treat your best suppliers as well as you treat your best customers. By building close relationships with your suppliers you can use them for feedback and overseas market information – perhaps even some useful introductions.

You should share your exporting plans with your key suppliers, because both parties need to be aware of any limiting factors (like tooling restrictions).

## Member Organisations

As well as the Chambers of Commerce, there are other general member organisations whose members can be useful sources of information. The Federation of Small Businesses (FSB) and the Institute of Directors (IOD) spring to mind, but there are others.

Do not be afraid to ask for help, you will be surprised how much knowledge is around.

## Sector-Specific Support

You may belong to organisations which are open only to businesses within a sector (agricultural, pharmaceutical, automotive etc). The members of such organisations may already have experience of exporting items similar to yours and it may even suit all parties for you to share representatives. Whilst taking time to find out who can help, you should take care, however, not to broadcast your export plans to your competitors!

## Banks

Before you start exporting, especially if you are going to get involved with foreign currency transactions or Letters Of

Credit, you should have a chat with your bank. Tell them which countries you are planning to deal with and discuss the implications of the various methods of payment.

The banks can provide some useful country guides, in which they identify financial forecasts and trends. They can also warn of any potential credit risks.

**Credit Insurers**

As I mentioned earlier on, the best way of dealing with export customers is on a Cash In Advance basis, but this will not please your customers and they may also baulk at the thought of using Letters Of Credit. If you are to proceed by using Open Account terms, I strongly advise that you only do so if you can secure credit insurance. The feedback you receive from credit insurers is very useful.

I rarely obtained Cash In Advance terms (usually only from previous poor payers) and, if insurance was unavailable, I insisted on Letters Of Credit (confirmed by a U.K. bank).

Credit insurers usually issue bulletins which flag early if particular countries are likely to present credit risks. I soon became nervous if credit insurance was not forthcoming, especially if the country concerned was not on our list of usual suspects.

Never forget that if you don't get paid, everything that has gone before was a complete waste of time and money. By being seen to run a tight ship, you will probably get plenty of respect from your customers.

**Trading Standards**

Your local Trading Standards people will be able to give you advice on safety labelling and similar requirements.

## Regulatory Bodies

If your products need particular approvals before they can be sold in the UK, they will almost certainly need something similar in your export market. Sometimes your representative can help you with this but don't be afraid to ask your U.K. regulatory body for advice regarding the process and the length of time it might take.

## Packaging Consultants

If your products are going to be delivered to far-flung destinations after being handled by several agencies, they may well need more sturdy and protective packaging. On the other hand, if they are going via a container, door-to-door, then your standard U.K. packaging may well suffice.

You need to take advice from a packaging consultant, after having established how your goods will be shipped (road, rail, sea, air). But it isn't just the sturdiness of the packaging to consider. You need to understand what external labelling is required by your export market customs authorities, the rail operator, the courier etc. Do not guess, otherwise you may end up with goods which are damaged or held up.

## GDPR Consultants

If you are planning to hold data in your export market, or data which refers to individuals in your export market, it would make sense to talk with a GDPR consultant before you get too far down the line.

## Translators

Perhaps you will produce exhibition material, sales literature, technical information or other printed matter in foreign languages. If any of these items are produced using inaccurate, offensive or amateurish translations, there is a real risk that you will start your export journey on the wrong foot.

Resist the temptation to use friends, family or free-of-charge online translation services. If you are going to produce something in the customer's language, get it done properly and use professionals. But, be careful – you don't need to get everything translated. If you are doing business through distributors or resellers, all you need on your website is a link to their websites, you don't need to translate the whole of your front page.

**Specialist Export Advisers**

In addition to all the other sources of advice, you could use specialist export advisers. But I would say that, wouldn't I? I spent a number of years working across a range of sectors, helping folks to avoid the mistakes I had made or witnessed over the years.

Such advice is not free but it comes from someone who has been on the journey you are just beginning. They can help you to stay on track and should be able to help you around any roadblocks.

Keep your eyes open for appropriate conferences, presentations, seminars etc. There are lots of events covering specific parts of the world (Middle East, South America, China and so on) and others which cover particular aspects of international trade (Letters Of Credit, Export Pricing, Exhibiting Overseas and others). At these events you will learn a lot, you will meet experts and you can network with fellow exporters.

So, exporting need not be the lonely challenge that it sometimes appears. There is help available all over the place and there are countless businesses around who can share their exporting experiences with you. All you need then is an enormous amount of stamina and, dare I say it, some good fortune. If you listen to advice and if you are prepared to put in the necessary hard work, exporting can be an enjoyable and profitable activity.

# 15. BRITISH EXPORTERS'
# BIGGEST MISTAKES

If everything seems under control, you're just not going fast enough (Mario Andretti)

I always choose a lazy person to do a hard job because a lazy person will find an easy way to do it (Bill Gates)

The person who invented Autocorrect should burn in hello (Tim Vine)

Having spent the whole of this book telling you what to do, it seems only right that I should finish the book by telling you what <u>not</u> to do. Over the years I have come across some excellent exporters, people who have built very successful export businesses in a profitable and sustainable way. As well as doing all the things I have recommended in this book, they have also shown creativity and have taken calculated risks. Even these successful exporters have made mistakes along the way but they have learned from those mistakes and applied those lessons to future activities.

I have also come across some unsuccessful exporters, who have managed to get things wrong. Unsuccessful exporters all have one thing in common – they think it is everyone else's fault and never their own. I have broken down the mistakes exporters make into seven categories:-

## 1. Inappropriate Product

If you are looking to achieve export sales, you need to be offering something which is designed, manufactured or grown locally. I have seen some people try to export products which they themselves have imported from another country. Think about it – if you have imported something from China and then you re-export it to Belgium, your Belgian customer will end up paying a much higher price than if the product was bought directly from China. So, why would they want to buy from you?

You may be offering something which is very acceptable in the U.K., but it is only going to be a "niche" proposition in other markets. The reasons could be climatic, religious, political or practical and you end up with a position simply too difficult with which to persevere.

## 2. Wrong Target Market

I have often heard "Oh, Mike, I am going to start exporting and I am going to start in China, because it is the biggest market in the world". No, it isn't – it has one of the two largest populations in the world, but that is not the same as saying it is the biggest market. Only about 2 or 3% of Chinese can afford Western products at Western prices, which makes China similar in size to the Benelux region, or Scandinavia – and China is much tougher to manage than those two areas.

I spent a couple of weeks in China a while back, along with eleven other export advisers from the U.K. We met with local businesses, local chambers, the Chinese partners of British law firms and also with British companies who were successfully doing business in China. My conclusion was that selling to China is not for the faint-hearted and needs to be fully thought through.

The most common mistake I encounter is where people have decided to target the U.S.A., purely because they speak English and they appear to have a similar culture. As chapter 12 of this book explains, the American business culture is very different from European business culture and British exporters need to make a number of changes before they look at America. I have seen more British fingers burned in America than anywhere else.

Perhaps the most difficult one for me has been to advise against businesses who have decided to sell to the homeland of their parents or grandparents. This often happens with business owners who come from Indian or Pakistani backgrounds. They understand the language, the culture and the religion, so they think that those markets should be logical targets for their British commercial propositions. I once worked with raincoat manufacturers, whose obvious target markets were places like Ireland, Belgium and Denmark. But they listened to their parents instead of to me and decided to supply the Indian raincoat market through their cousin in Chennai.

Mention of India reminds me of a meeting I attended in Dubai during early 1993, a time which coincided with an England cricket tour of India. Before the tour started, there had been controversy when England's star batsman, David Gower, had been omitted from the squad. The tour started badly and every newspaper was saying "You should have taken Gower". During the meeting, we received a polished presentation from a director of Godrej in India. He finished up his talk by stating "I only have one more thing to add. Mike Stokes, you should have taken Gower".

## 3. Impatience

I have often mentioned that exporting takes time, it is not a quick fix. Whenever I have started to mentor new exporters, I have tried to manage their expectations. If you are starting out on the export road, you need to understand the various steps and how long they will take.

The lack of patience is usually caused by two culprits, the Managing Director and the Financial Director. Often, I have been approached by Sales Directors who told me that their MD has instructed them to achieve certain export targets within something like 6 months. The first thing I did then was to meet with the MD and I explained what they were walking into. Eventually I walked out with a more sensible plan, but, even then, the impatience could be a real problem.

FDs become an obstacle when they refuse to sanction business trips. "Why are you going there again? You didn't get any orders last time." Once you have become established and you are producing profits, then the FD will realise the benefit of your earlier patience. But in the early days they can be a frustrating barrier to your success.

A downturn in the domestic market can result in more resources being thrown at the local problem, which can result in the export project being delayed. As a result, people become impatient and lose focus.

## 4. Failure to Research

Some businesses start out on their export journey without reference to any of the support organisations I mentioned. They therefore fail to pick up on the need for research. As a result, they end up in the wrong markets, with inappropriate product offerings, alongside the wrong partners and probably with naïve pricing.

Some people pay "lip service" to researching and they end up doing only half a job. Every piece of data gleaned through research should be verified by using another piece of research, from an unrelated source.

I have attended trade shows over the years where my fellow British exhibitors on adjacent stands clearly had not done their research. The local attendees (who could be potential trading partners) can spot those who have not researched, and the opportunity is lost.

My colleague once placed an advertisement in the Irish press for a training manager in "Southern Ireland". We were surprised that we only received applications from places like Cork, Waterford and Wexford. That is because the Irish themselves refer to their country as "Republic of Ireland", just "Ireland" or the "Twenty Six counties". Any reference to

"Southern Ireland" is interpreted as the towns on or near the south coast of the island.

## 5. Wrong Route to Market

In some cases, I have seen exporters who have the right product for the right market – but they have chosen the wrong route to market. For instance, if your product is perishable with a very short shelf life, a traditional route of *supplier – wholesaler – retailer – customer* may have too many links in the chain. As a result, your products will be in a bad state when they arrive with the customer. Cutting out one or more link may solve the problem, but the answer may have to be a franchising/licensing/JV arrangement so that your items are produced locally.

Similarly, if every one of the items you produce is customised (bespoke), then using an agent will probably be more effective than using a distributor or reseller.

## 6. Scattergun Approach

I have long advocated the strategy of being excellent in a small number of markets, rather than being mediocre in a large number of markets. Whenever exporters have told me that they need lots of new agents or distributors, I have invariably got them to spend more time doing a better job with their existing partners. The "scattergun" approach to exporting is ok for the pins affixed to your wall map but does little for your time management or for your profits.

I spent many hours helping a software business in Lincolnshire to draw up a detailed plan for their entry into the American market. This involved exhibiting at a trade fair in Los Angeles, making contact with businesses identified as likely resellers by UKTI's local research and arranging follow-up meetings after the trade fair. All this was contained

in a plan which was supported by matched funding from
UKTI. Two days after our last meeting, he called me to say
that he had a chance to visit India and was flying out before
the weekend. This was on the back of no discussions, no
research and no plan. Suffice it to say that he received no
funding for his Indian jaunt!

## 7. Unbalanced Four Ps

At the end of chapter 3, I pointed out the importance of
balancing your four Ps, the need to get all your Ps positioned
at the same level. I am afraid that many exporters fail to
realise their potential because they have proceeded with
unbalanced Ps.

One of the most common failures comes from the fact that
exporters think they can command the same prices in export
markets where their brand and products are unknown.

Another mistake is failing to realise the amount of
promotional expenditure needed to establish a brand in new
markets.

In some cases the choice of representative may be flawed. A
chosen organisation may not have the influence they said
they had to penetrate the desired market segment.

If things are not working out in a particular market, don't
forget to plot the positioning of your four Ps against your
competitors. See what they are doing right and see what you
are doing wrong. Then put together a plan to address the
problem.

# APPENDIX

The only place where success comes before work is in the dictionary. (Vince Lombardi)

Progress comes from the intelligent use of experience. (Albert Green Hubbard)

In the space age, man will be able to go around the world in two hours – one hour for flying and one hour to get to the airport. (Neil H. McElroy)

I have already made the point that I was paid to do a job, not act as a tourist. I therefore often missed the landmarks for which cities or countries are known, as my mission was to get from airports, to meeting locations, and then back again – in the shortest time and at the minimum cost.

I therefore failed to visit a number of famous places, despite having been within a few miles of them. Places such as the Leaning Tower of Pisa, the Blarney Stone, Patpong in Bangkok, La Scala in Milan, the Palace of Versailles and the Dead Sea.

I only saw New York from the air, as I once changed planes at JFK airport. In fact, New York is one of several cities which I have only seen whilst changing planes – the others being Gdansk, Stuttgart, Doha, Qingdao (Tsingtao) and Denpasar (Bali)

Many was the time that my evening meal consisted of a room service snack while I worked away on my laptop. Sometimes all I could get were a packet of crisps and a muesli bar from a vending machine.

However, I have been lucky enough to stay in some fabulous hotels, eat in some wonderful restaurants and work with some inspiring people. I would like to indulge myself therefore by sharing a few lists from my travels. I have not seen these places through the eyes of a travel company representative, so it is not recommended that you book your next holiday based upon one of my business trips. Neither should you book concert tickets on the basis of my chance encounters with celebrities.

**Famous Faces (Music)**

I was walking through Gatwick Airport very early one Sunday morning, with hardly anyone about, when I came face to face with someone I recognised. I did a double take, which caught his eye, but then his face dropped when he realised it was just another oik who had recognised him. The next time I saw **Eric Clapton** was during one of his legendary concerts at the Albert Hall.

I was awaiting a flight home from Athens and sat quietly in the business class lounge. In came two people I recognised, **Steve Harris** and **Dave Murray** from the band Iron Maiden. Disappointingly, they sipped Perrier water and read the Financial Times. I just wanted them to chuck the TV out of the window, like rock stars are supposed to!

Waiting one evening at the baggage carousel at Heathrow, there was a tall, long-haired man rebelliously smoking a cigarette immediately under the "No Smoking" sign. It was Led Zeppelin's singer, **Robert Plant**. As we were big fans, I phoned my wife to tell her and she said "well put your phone down, go over and get his autograph". I approached him and got his signature on the back of my business card and I can report what a really nice guy he was. After I had returned to the carousel, I noticed several other business people in suits approaching Robert.

While changing planes at Stuttgart, I noticed that the little chap (5 feet 7 inches) standing next to me on the shuttle bus was the jazz legend, **Acker Bilk**. He was with a group of folks, so I didn't get chance to speak with him.

I was waiting for my luggage at Thessaloniki airport and I noticed what was obviously a team of roadies, handling amplifiers, instruments and monitors. I asked them who they were with and they told me they were working with the former Rolling Stones guitarist, **Mick Taylor**, who was playing in Thessaloniki that same evening. When I met my host, I convinced him that we should buy tickets and attend the concert – which we did. Unfortunately, the crowd kept asking for "Brown Sugar", which Mick didn't play with his blues band.

I mentioned earlier in the book that I got my Icelandic colleague introduced to the jazz performer, **Georgie Fame**. Georgie was very friendly and had plenty of time for my friend – and he had a fascinating mid-Atlantic accent, sort of where New York meets Leigh!

### Famous Faces (Entertainment)

I have already mentioned **Linda Pétursdóttir**, the reigning "Miss World", who sat next to me on a flight from Keflavik. I also bumped into a few other showbiz folks.

**The Krankies** were causing much mayhem (well, Jimmy was) at the British Midland check-in at Heathrow one Sunday evening. It helped to relieve the boredom as almost everyone's flights were delayed that evening.

Actress **Nanette Newman** and her film director husband **Bryan Forbes** shared an airport shuttle bus with my wife and I at Munich, on our way home from Malta.

The actors **Paul and Joe McGann** jumped the taxi queue outside Jury's Hotel in Dublin one morning – but no-one seemed to mind!

We had three celebrity chefs cooking at one of our London trade shows and I got to meet all of them – **Brian Turner, James Martin and Lesley Waters.**

Similarly, I had a chat with chef **Michael Barry** on the Kenwood stand at an exhibition in Cologne.

I met **Oz Clarke**, the wine expert, in a hotel lift one day.

I bumped into the author **Jilly Cooper**, in the business class lounge at Dublin airport once. As a non-fiction reader, I was unable to give her any feedback on the many books she has written.

## Famous Faces (Sport)

At a very busy Sunday morning check-in at Heathrow, golfer **Nick Faldo** was very grumpy because they wouldn't let him and his skis jump the queue.

The chap holding the door for me at Manchester airport was none other than the England football captain, **Bryan Robson**.

Whilst waiting to leave Helsinki, I chatted with English FA officials, **Bert Millichip and Graham Kelly**.

Footballer and later manager of Nottingham Forest, **Frank Clark**, sat across the aisle from me on a flight to Belfast.

The F1 world champion, **James Hunt**, shared a hotel lift with me in Dublin on one occasion. He looked very disjointed, with no socks on, so you can only guess what he may have been up to!

I caught Northern Ireland goalkeeper, **Pat Jennings**, in the lounge at the Airport Hotel in Dublin. That was also the location where the whole Ireland football team gathered one Sunday evening, in the bar of course.

Dutch darts master, **Roland Scholten**, shared a flight to Amsterdam with me just after he had won a televised tournament.

**Alan Hansen**, the former Liverpool centre back and later football pundit, was sat at the next table to me at a Dublin restaurant.

Nigel Truswell and I were staying at a Tokyo hotel in December 1997, when the Intercontinental Cup was being played (at a stadium in Tokyo) between the German team Borussia Dortmund and Cruzeiro of Brazil. After the game, the Borussia team came into the hotel bar and their Scottish forward, **Scott Booth**, spent a while chatting to us.

Other sporting names I encountered were the **England Rugby Team of 1986** and the **Greece Basketball Team of 2001**. I flew with the English team and was surrounded by the giant Greeks in a hotel foyer.

I came close to meeting a World Cup legend during an exhibition. I was occupied talking to a customer, so I was unable to go across and speak to a gentleman queuing politely for one of our brochures. It was 1966 hero **Geoff Hurst**, working in insurance at that time.

### Famous Faces (Politics)

Two passengers put their names down for the waiting list for an earlier flight from Paris to London – myself and **David Owen**, the former SDP leader. He was taller than I expected and I was amused that the French check-in assistant didn't recognise a character who was on British TV very regularly at that time. "And what is your name, sir?" As it turned out, neither of us was called forward.

**Clement Freud** was smaller than I expected, although perhaps not in terms of girth.

And someone who was taller than I expected, and very purposeful with a strong-striding walk, was **Ian Paisley**. The way he marched through Heathrow suggested he was a man on a mission.

Sharing a hotel lift with me in Cork was **John Bruton**. At the time he was the Leader of the Opposition in Ireland but later he became Taoiseach (Prime Minister).

Sharing a flight to Gatwick with me in 1989 was the Maltese Prime Minister, **"Eddie" Fenech Adami**.

Perhaps the most memorable politician I met was **Antonis Samaras**. At the time I met him, he was the Greek Minister of Foreign Affairs and he spent several minutes on our stand at the 1991 Thessaloniki International Trade Fair. He took an interest in our Greek activity and said it was good to see that I travelled out there to support our local people. Between 2012 and 2015, Samaras was the Greek Prime Minister.

**Favourite Cities**

I visited **Dublin** more often than any other city and, despite its pretty awful weather, it remained my favourite. I have already commented on the hospitable, irreverent, chatty Irish people and it is the people that make Dublin so special.

Towards the end of my time visiting Dublin, I was flying home one Friday evening and read the local evening paper. I picked up on an advert in the sports section, advertising a meeting of the "Dublin Clarets" at a local pub. A supporters branch of my beloved Burnley FC in Dublin! I contacted the group and attended quite a few of their monthly meetings over the next 18 months, managing to arrange many of my business meetings to coincide with the meetings of the Dublin Clarets.

No matter how many times I have visited **Paris**, I never tired of it. I only ever spoke "schoolboy" French but I managed to find my way around quite well. I just loved the whole ambience of Paris, with hardly a bad restaurant in the place.

There are many famous places in Paris, including the magnificent Louvre Museum and arts centre. I once had the pleasure of Evans' inimitable conducted tour of the place – which must have taken all of 50 minutes!

On one occasion, Nigel Truswell and I were meeting a candidate for a sales position and we agreed to conduct an informal interview with him in a bar near the Gare du Nord. I say "informal" because we already knew him and he was the obvious candidate to choose. To cut a long story short, we didn't realise that he couldn't take his drink, and he was too polite to refuse. Fortunately we had time to offer him the job before he became totally blotto!

As a result of an unfortunate misunderstanding, our French distributor booked Evans and myself into the prestigious George V hotel – the one that has been used over the years by pop stars, politician and visiting royalty. We realised the error as soon as we checked in, so we concocted a cock and bull story to enable us to check out after one night and not incur any penalty charges (I think I had a sick relative or something). The cost of everything there was phenomenal and, upon checking out, Evans remarked "I was afraid to fart in case they charged me."

I have only been to **Sydney** twice, but that was all I needed to add it to my list of favourite cities. And my memories of the two visits are very different.

On both occasions, I enjoyed really positive and well-structured business meetings. The Australians are excellent to deal with – tough negotiators but they deliver what they promise. But after my two meetings, the experiences were very different.

After the meeting on my first visit, I was treated to a night-time Sydney harbour cruise with views of the Southern Cross and the unforgettable Opera House. But the memory I loved was cruising slowly under the Sydney Harbour Bridge under the stars.

On my second visit, after the meeting it was suggested that I should visit some local retailers – and we finished that by 4.30pm on a Friday afternoon. That is when all inhabitants of Sydney seem to descend on their local bars to start the weekend.

The Aussies are of course great cricket lovers. After a very long evening, I demonstrated how I could bowl a leg break with enough turn to go around the corner of the pub. It seemed a good idea at the time! The following morning I could not remember the taxi ride back to my hotel, but I somehow had a receipt in my pocket!

I will always have a soft spot for **Thessaloniki**. My first "day" there ended up with me driving my host's car at 4am because he was too sleepy. There are excellent fish restaurants, ice cream parlours and salad bars, all with the warmest of welcomes. My visits there often resulted in visits to bazuki clubs, complete with loud emotional music and individual dramatic dances. In those days, they were still allowed to smash plates but I believe *"Health And Safety"* have since banned the practice. One of the clubs I visited had a car park, the surface of which was made up of smashed plate fragments.

I have fond memories of delivering dealer presentations in Halkidiki, which is within driving distance of Thessaloniki. My hosts were proud Macedonians who were only too keen to teach me about local customs – and every story seemed to include Alexander the Great.

I was lucky in that my employer was very early to use laptop computers and mobile phones. And, because I travelled more than anyone else, I always got the new gadgets first. I must have been one of the first passengers to go through Thessaloniki airport with a mobile phone and my phone caused interference with the tannoy system, so embarrassingly I was asked to turn it off.

**Memorable Cities**

Having shared my four favourite cities, I have to declare also those places which are not my favourites but are still memorable.

I felt a bit of a fraud when I first visited **Jerusalem**. Although I found it very interesting historically, my parents would have got so much more from the visit. I do not share my parents' faith but I do respect what they believed and they would have found the whole thing so uplifting. You cannot fail to be impressed by the place, and I believe we should all be made to visit Yad Vashem, the Holocaust History Museum.

During my first visit to Jerusalem, a small party of us were allowed to visit **Bethlehem**, which is in Palestine (the West Bank). I went into the Church of the Nativity, which my parents would have found so inspiring. Even then, the place was tense and there were Israeli soldiers everywhere. I believe that access is now a problem.

**Tokyo** is the most vibrant city I have visited. There is a real buzz about the place and despite the huge volume of people and vehicles, it is all so well organised.

The Japanese are not easy to deal with, partly because they think you will be offended if they say "no". They also use long periods of silence, not to intimidate you but because they are thinking. Having said that, they are extremely polite and they do what they say they will do. Once the brief cases have been closed, the Japanese like to let their hair down and karaoke is almost compulsory.

One of the most attractive cities I have seen is **Vienna**. It has some really lovely buildings and, the first time I went there, I stayed near the Schönbrunn Palace. Completing the "naughty" tour of the coffee houses and cake shops is very enjoyable – but poor for your waistline. Vienna is a must for fans of classical music and it is a bit wasted on an uncouth rock and blues fan like me.

**Barcelona** was a pleasant place to visit and to do business but my most vivid memory of the place was being close to getting hit by lightning! Evans and I were on our way back to our hotel after our first meeting, probably about midday. Suddenly the heavens opened and everyone rushed into shop and office doorways to escape the torrential rain. While we were sheltering, a huge and loud lightning bolt hit the dome of the church on the opposite corner of the square. There was a tense electric feel for some minutes afterwards and it is the closest I have come to being struck.

I only visited **Buenos Aires** once. The visit started tensely, as I had gone there to placate a very unhappy distributor. But, as the atmosphere lightened, I got to witness the other side of the city, culminating in a magnificent steak dinner in the city centre. Buenos Aires on a Saturday night was certainly very lively.

There was one scary moment during my stay in Buenos Aires. One morning I went into the bathroom and discovered a creature at the bottom of the shower. I can only describe it as a cross between a large beetle and a king prawn. I had no idea whether it was poisonous or not, but I decided to take no chances. I demolished it with a single blow of the heel of my shoe. I know that was not very noble of me – but needs must!

## Memorable Structures

Although the Sydney Opera House quite rightly receives lots of attention, it was the **Sydney Harbour Bridge** that impressed me most. I got to walk over the bridge during my second visit there and I always like to see how they use the bridge for New Year firework displays. I was entertained at the foot of the bridge by a fascinating array of street artists, jugglers and mime artists.

I never did manage to visit the **Eiffel Tower** during any of my business visits until the week I combined a business trip with a short break in Paris with my wife. The view from the top is spectacular, helped by the fact that we were there long before the global obsession with "selfies".

It wasn't until my thirteenth visit to Athens that I got to visit the **Acropolis**. One of my afternoon meetings was postponed, so I found myself as a tourist for the rest of the day. I was the only person not dressed in tee shirt and shorts in the blistering heat – but at least I made it.

I have fond memories of Cologne and I often walked over one of the Rhine bridges after long days spent on exhibition stands. The magnificent night-time view of **Cologne Cathedral** was memorable.

Jerusalem was a very interesting place to visit and I was allowed to get up close to the Western Wall (also known by Christians as the Wailing Wall). But the most spectacular sight is the **Golden Dome** (or the Dome Of The Rock) behind the Western Wall. The Dome sits so proudly above this city which is significant to a number of different faiths.

During a visit to Bangkok, I was taken to see the gold-plated **Reclining Buddha**, which is 46 metres long.

## Memorable Countrysides

The landscape in **Iceland** is like nothing else I have seen, maybe like visiting the Moon. I was lucky enough to have been taken by car on a gloriously sunny day to see The Great Geysir, Gullfoss Waterfall, various hot springs and mountains with steam gushing from their sides. On another trip, I flew to Akureyri, across mile upon mile of glaciers. Spectacular scenery in a country where they can have all four seasons in one day!

I mentioned earlier in the book that I took a really picturesque train journey between Vienna and Salzburg in **Austria**. Rugged mountains, tumbling streams and chocolate box villages helped to make this a delightful journey.

Similarly, I remember a spectacular train journey in **Norway**, between Gol and Oslo. Norway is beautiful in June and the passengers lapped up the scenery. Unfortunately, the train driver must have loved the scenery as well, because we arrived in Oslo very late – so late that I only just caught my flight, but my luggage followed on the next day!

Most of my views of **Switzerland** have been from the air, flying over the spectacular Alps on my way to Greece or Turkey. But on my few business trips there (Geneva, Montreux and Zurich) I found a very attractive mix of beautiful scenery and extremely clean cities. It also helped that the Swiss are such efficient people to deal with.

## Eyesores

Over the years I discovered places which were less than easy on the eye. I apologise if this list offends anyone, but I can only speak as I find.

Back in the mid 1980s, the citizens of **Malta** found that they could pick up a number of Italian TV stations if they used very tall aerials. So my first impression of this wonderfully-hospitable island was row upon row of tall, ugly aerials.

When arriving in France by ferry from Dover, the first thing you see is the drab, grey view of **Calais**. Perhaps I was unlucky with the weather whenever I used Calais, but it never seemed any different.

I first went to **Bilbao** in the late 1980s, before they started to spend money on the place's appearance. It really was not a pretty sight in those days, contrasting markedly with the glorious scenery inland, towards Mondragon.

The worst road I have travelled was the main road between the city of **Wuhan** (China) and its airport. Our bus driver had to make substantial detours around the biggest potholes I have witnessed. Some of the holes were no worse than those in Fenland but some of them were frightening chasms.

On a car journey between Brno and Vienna, I caught the ring road around **Bratislava**. To be frank, it looked like one big industrial park, with chimneys billowing all sorts of stuff into the atmosphere.

I visited Ukraine on two occasions, staying on the second visit at a pleasant hotel in Kiev. My first visit was to **Donetsk**, in the east of the country. The hotel I was booked into was quite the worst I have ever used. I actually spread my overcoat over my bed as it was filthy, the door had holes knocked into it, and the plumbing was hideous. The people were fine, and the hotel was probably the best one they had, but it was grim.

**Gibraltar** was a place which I would not recommend. It was interesting to see how "hollow" the Rock itself is, but I found the town to be shabby and pretty depressing.

As a "treat" on my final day in **Bangkok**, I was taken on a tour of the city in a motorised gondola. The boat went in and out of every branch of the river, opening my eyes to the appalling squalor in which people were living. I feared that if I had fallen overboard I would never have survived, judging from the stuff I saw floating in the water.

My tour continued by car and included a trip to an enormous crocodile farm. It was very hot and very humid and, inappropriately, I was wearing a very sweaty replica football top.

My hosts in Bangkok were excellent but I found the place unnerving. It was impossible for me, as an obviously visiting Western businessman, to sit on my own in a bar for more than 5 minutes without being asked if I wanted some "company" for the evening.

And that brings me to my most disliked place, **Jakarta**. I only ever went there once and I have already described my visa problem there. I took a taxi from the airport to my hotel and after a mile or two, I was aware that the roadway was filling up, apparently with people finishing work for the day. As well as the intense feeling of claustrophobia, I felt very vulnerable, as an obvious foreigner on his own in a cab which was surrounded by people. The journey took ages and I was extremely relieved to arrive at my hotel.

I had an unsatisfactory meeting with the local distributor and then, on my second evening in Jakarta, I had a long and very interesting chat with a Qantas airline pilot. As we were leaving, he pointed out that we were the only men in that bar who had not been "befriended" during the evening. I apologised if I had cramped his style and left!

## Worst Airport Landings

I have no fear when an aeroplane takes off, nor do I have a problem when it is cruising. But I am not overly keen on landings. Not being an engineer, I don't understand why the landing gear doesn't just crumple under the weight of a landing plane every time.

Some of the most precarious landings I have experienced include the following:-

The old Kai Tak airport at **Hong Kong** used to frighten me to death. The plane had to bank quite severely as it approached the runway, in order to miss the high rise buildings all around. Seeing faces in the windows of nearby apartments was scary enough, but then you felt the enormous burst of reverse thrust as the plane just about halted before the end of the runway. Thankfully, a new airport is now operating.

I always hate those airport approaches where you can see nothing but sea all around you until the very last few seconds. One of the worst for this is **Larnaca** in Cyprus.

Another airport where you are not aware of the runway until very late is **London City Airport**. All you can see is high rise buildings and converted docks until you hit the deck.

But the most hair-raising of all was **Gibraltar**. The runway there is short and it crosses the main road between Gibraltar town and Spain. So, the traffic on the main road is brought to a halt as the plane comes down, the plane hits the deck and then brakes really heavily to avoid falling off the end of the runway. There is nothing they can do about it, as the runway can only run for the width of the isthmus. And if they turned it round by 90 degrees, there is a dirty great rock in the way!

## Best Food

As someone who spent many hours living off airport snacks and vending machine food, why am I qualified to comment on food? Probably because many hours travelling make you appreciate good food when you eventually get some. Some of the most memorable meals I have had were not particularly expensive – just tasty.

**Mussels (Belgium)** – Evans introduced me to *moules et frites* at the Chez Léon restaurant in Brussels. I have tasted mussels at many other places but those were the best I had, marginally better than those served up in Galway.

**Dorada (Spain)** – "Gilt Head Bream" (or "Golden Fish") in English was a salt-baked fish served at the "La Dorada" restaurant in Madrid. When helped down with glasses of Viña Sol, it was an outstanding experience.

**Couscous Royale (France)** – this was my first taste of couscous at Chez Bébert, one of the many excellent North African restaurants in Paris. I went there with Evans during my second or third trip to Paris, and I have since taken my wife there.

**Beef Steak (Argentina)** – it will surely be no surprise when I nominate Argentinian steak as the best I have tasted. I am not a big steak lover, but that was exceptional. After a very successful meeting I was able to experience great food at a very lively downtown restaurant in Buenos Aires. The portion was plentiful and delicious.

**Sacher Torte (Austria)** – this is one of Vienna's most famous desserts and I sampled it at the Viennese coffee house which bears its name. Naughty but nice!

**Soda Bread (Ireland)** – while travelling in Ireland, I often used to stop at rural pubs at lunchtime for home-made soup (or chowder) and a sandwich. The local soda bread was delicious – it also goes really well with mussels.

**Salmon (Iceland)** – I am a great lover of salmon and my wife's salmon risotto is my favourite meal. Away from home, the finest salmon I tasted was in Iceland. The Icelanders have a big reputation for good quality salmon, and I think it is well deserved.

**Onion Basket (Louisville, USA)** – sorry if this is bit down market, but it really was superb! It was a series of onion rings, woven together to form the shape of a basket. And being in the USA, it was a big boy's portion.

**Anything (Rouen)** – we appointed a distributor of spare parts to support our activity in France and their premises were on the south side of Rouen. We did not visit them very often, but we would always arrange an early start so that our meeting would finish by midday. Without fail, we were always taken out by our hosts for the most marvellous lunches you could dream up. Imaginative main courses, naughty desserts, a large selection of local cheeses and the very best wine to wash it all down. And lovely people too.

**Worst Food**

In life, you take the rough with the smooth and the same is true in export. As well as enjoying some wonderful food around the world, I have also had to put up with some awful stuff – partly because that was all there was to eat, and partly because I did not wish to offend my hosts.

I have already mentioned the **Pig's Ear Soup** at Santarem in Portugal. I recall that the soup also contained some fairly large stones – for effect, not for consumption.

During my first visit to Poland, I was taken to a restaurant in a heavily-wooded area just outside Poznan. There was apparently only one thing on the menu and it was called **golonka**, a large portion of practically inedible pork knuckle. Amongst the British exhibitors at an overly-long trade show, "golonka" was our greeting for the rest of our time there. That was another occasion when I had to raid the vending kiosk near my hotel when I returned.

On my second visit to Iceland, I was assured that the starter at our meal was a "popular local delicacy". It was a small portion of **whale**, which was slimey and difficult to keep down. Never again!

I am very lucky in having a strong constitution, hardly ever do I get tummy upsets and I have never done what Steven Marshall did in Tokyo – he suddenly went running into a restaurant just to use the loo after something upset him. The only time I suffered on my travels was the day after eating **turkey schnitzel** in Cologne. The restaurant had been immaculate and the last place you would imagine to give you food poisoning. But I suffered for half a day!

I have already said that during my stay in **Donetsk**, my hotel was the worst I experienced. Well, so was the food! I was in Ukraine not too long after the Soviet Union had split up and I appreciated that they had not exactly enjoyed the good life, in terms of food. But just about everything my colleagues and I were given was gross, so I usually found myself just eating the bread. We had been warned in advance not to eat the salad as it had been washed in the local water. Again, nice people who probably gave us the best they had.

## Best Drinks

I hope that this book has not made me come across as an alcoholic, but I recognise that alcoholic drinks have featured quite prominently in some of my anecdotes. I never had a drink before or during a customer meeting and obviously couldn't drink on my flight home because I had a car to drive. But many of my hosts liked a drink after a meeting and especially with a meal. I also spent many hours in airport lounges and hotel bars with only a book for company. So, I liked a drink when it was appropriate.

Travelling to Ireland as often as I did, it was inevitable that I would develop a liking for **Guinness**. I really liked the stuff, but rarely touched it back in Great Britain. Generally speaking, British bar staff are inadequately trained in how to keep, pour and serve Guinness and it is not the same experience.
The best Irish pubs for Guinness in my time were Ryan's of Parkgate Street (Dublin), the Hole in the Wall (Castleknock, Dublin) and Durty Nelly's (Bunratty, Limerick). I enjoyed many happy hours at these places.

My distributor in Belgium part-owned a popular brewery in Antwerp called **De Koninck**. It was available throughout Belgium but I was treated one evening to a tour of the brewery, followed by a couple of glasses at the bar across the road which had a direct line in from the brewery. Absolute nectar!

Until I visited Australia, I really wasn't familiar with their local wines. When we went out with our hosts, they insisted that as well as quaffing the local VB beer, we should get to know their wines. It was then that I fell in love with **Australian Shiraz**, and it has been a regular in my wine rack since.

In the early 1990s, Hotpoint started to collaborate with the French manufacturer, Thomson Brandt, and the Spanish manufacturer, Fagor. My involvement with Fagor necessitated my travelling quite often to their headquarters at Mondragon, located in a beautiful area of the Basque region. It was my Basque hosts who introduced me to **Rioja** red wine – especially supplied by Cune. I have regarded this ever since as my favourite red wine.

Some drinks I have had just hit a spot as they were taken at exactly the right time. I am thinking about Cisk beer consumed on a warm Maltese afternoon, complimentary tawny Port served at the hotel check-in at Porto after a long journey and piping hot Espresso coffee after travelling to Fabriano (Italy) through a snowstorm. All were very welcome!

**Worst Drinks**

To balance out this part of the book, I felt that I should also nominate the worst drinks I experienced on my travels.

First place, without hesitation, goes to **Ouzo**. This is a very well-known and seemingly popular drink, which all visitors to Greece feel obliged to taste. I think that the flavour is absolutely horrible.

Although Czech beer is excellent, the Czechs feature twice in my "Worst" list. I mentioned earlier in the book that Evans and I were invited out to a local wine tasting evening. We politely said how nice the **Czech white wine** was but in reality it was diabolical.

Some years later, I visited Prague with a team of UKTI staff for a meeting with the local team, based at the British Embassy. It coincided with a walk around the Christmas Fair and someone in our party decided to buy a large glass of

**mulled Czech wine** for each of us. It was gruesome stuff and I ended up pouring mine down a drain. My colleague, Bob O'Meara, said "I saw what you did there. Mine had already gone the same way two minutes ago".

# INDEX

Management is doing things right. Leadership is doing the right things (Peter Drucker)

A successful man is one who can lay a firm foundation with the bricks others have thrown at him (David Brinkley)

A verbal contract isn't worth the paper it's written on (Samuel Goldwyn)

Daikin 54

Danish 106

DBT 144, 145

Dead Sea

De Konink 179

Denmark 156

Denpasar (Bali) 161

Dockers 117

Doha 161

Dome Of The Rock 171, 172

Donetsk 173, 178

Dos Santos, Luis 40

Dubai 24, 84, 110

Dublin 33, 113, 115, 117, 120, 135, 139, 163, 164, 166, 179

"Dublin Clarets" 166

Dudley, Sarah 135, 136

Dundalk 116

Durty Nelly's 179

Dutch 39, 97, 113, 164

Duval 34

**E**

East Midlands 9

Edwards, Oliver 115, 116, 118

Egypt 18

Eiffel Tower 109, 171

Ellis Island 123

England Rugby Team 165

Espresso 180

Essex 9

Evans, Pat 14

Evans, Stuart 12-14, 41, 75, 78, 79, 109, 111, 167, 170, 176

"Export Times" 16

Exportential 9

**F**

Fabriano 180

Faeroes 18

Fagor 180

Faldo, Nick 164

Fame, Georgie 85, 163

"Father Ted" 117

Fenland 173

"Financial Times" 162

Finland 37

Finnish 33

Fisher 54

Flemish 18

Forbes, Bryan 163

France 26, 68, 173, 176, 177

Taffies 115

Taoiseach 166

Taylor, Mick 162, 163

Tel Aviv 76

Thessaloniki 32, 82, 107, 162, 166, 168, 169

Thomson Brandt 75, 180

Tokyo 24, 95, 165, 169, 178

Tone, Wolfe 114

Toshiba 82, 95

Transparency International 41

Truswell, Nigel 127, 128, 165, 167

Turkey 172

Turkish 53

Turner, Brian 163

Tyson, Mike 13

**U**

USP 27

U.S.A. 24, 39, 53, 67, 115, 119, 120, 123, 124, 126, 127, 155, 177

U2 12, 117

Ukraine 47, 77, 173, 178

Utrecht 111

**V**

Valletta 11

Vienna 77, 170, 172,173,177

Vina Sol 176

Voltaire 12

**W**

Wailing Wall 171

Wales 12

Wardell, Bob 138

Warsaw 79

Waterford 157

Waters, Lesley 163

Wedgwood 78

Weinstock, Lord 7

Welch, Dennis 120

Welch, Jack 7, 8

Welsh 12, 84, 115

Wembley 12

West Cork 115

Western Wall 171

Wexford 157

White, Graham 7, 20

Wuhan 173

**Y**

Yad Vashem 169

**Z**

Zurich 172

# BY THE SAME AUTHOR

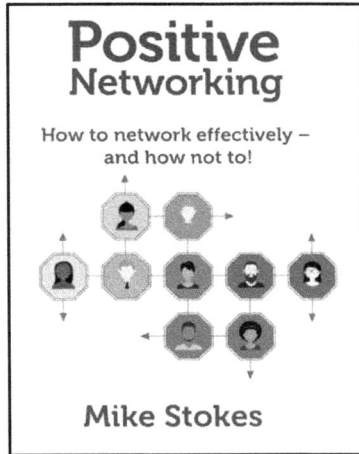

**Positive**
**Networking**

How to network effectively –
and how not to!

**Mike Stokes**

Business networking has become an increasingly important element within the marketing strategy of a business but, like all marketing activities, it needs to be planned, structured and measured if it is to be effective.

Having been a prolific networker and the creator of innovative networking events over a number of years, Mike Stokes has seen some of the best networkers in action – and some of the worst!

This book helps new and inexperienced business networkers to
- find the most appropriate networking groups for their businesses
- understand how to network effectively
- recognise the mistakes that poor networkers make

It also assists organisers of networking events by
- outlining how to establish and grow a networking group
- suggesting ways in which rounds of elevator pitches can be spiced up
- explaining how to set up and run 20 different networking formats

The book introduces networkers to The 5 Ps of Networking and it gives leaders of networking groups a stack of new ideas.

If your networking is NOT working, it is almost certainly your own fault, and this book explains why.

Milton Keynes UK
Ingram Content Group UK Ltd.
UKHW020749111223
434160UK00016B/860